Everything You Didn't Need To Know About The

Printed and bound in Great Britain by Butler & Tanner Ltd, Frome, Somerset

Distributed in the US by Publishers Group West

Published by Sanctuary Publishing Limited, Sanctuary House,
45–53 Sinclair Road, London W14 0NS, United Kingdom

www.sanctuarypublishing.com

Cover concept: Splashdown
Cover illustration: Peter Quinnell
Illustrations: Axos

'Flower Of Scotland'
Words by Roy Williamson
© The Corris (Music) Ltd

'Land Of My Fathers'
Words by Evan James

'God Save The Queen'
Words Anonymous

ISBN: 1-86074-597-0

Everything You
Didn't Need To
Know About The

Nick Brownlee

Sanctuary

PREFACE

'History is bunk', the American car manufacturer Henry Ford famously once said. It is difficult to disagree with him: in America, history is comparatively non-existent, stretching back barely 300 years. In terms of British history, 300 years is nothing. It is a drop in what is a vast, turbulent and, in parts, uncharted ocean. The history of Britain is almost as old as civilisation itself – although at times civilisation is the last thing the occupants of this small island could ever be accused of.

With Britain's history comes its rich and unique culture and outlook on life, which is often baffling to foreigners and even to folk who live in the next county. One cannot imagine, for example, Belgians chasing a rolling cheese downhill with the same gusto as people in Gloucestershire do every year. Similarly, where else but Ireland would you find an ancient monument not only situated in someone's garden, but blocking the front door so the occupants have to leave by the rear of the house?

The purpose of this book is to seek out and celebrate the quirks, idiosyncrasies and oddities that are so much a part of Britishness. We hope you enjoy it. Whether you believe it or not is a different matter entirely.

HAMPTON COURT MAZE

AN AIRPORT AND A HALF

Heathrow Airport was built as an aeroplane test base in 1929 and was a fighter base during World War II. It was converted for civilian use in 1946, and just seven years later more than a million passengers a year had passed through its terminals. There are now around 70 airlines from 61 countries flying more than 40 million passengers a year in and out of Heathrow – making it the world's busiest airport.

HOW TO TOSS A CABER

1 Stand with your heels together and toes out, with the narrow end of the caber on the ground between your feet.

2 The other athlete 'walks' it up (that is to say, he grabs the heavy end, raises it over his head and walks towards you until the caber is upright and right in your face).

3 Interlace your fingers almost to the palms, then get as much palm surface spread around the base as you can, dig the heels of your hands in as hard as you can, and *stand up*.

4 Using the upward moment imparted by your legs, drop your palms under the base of the caber.

5 Run, and then 'plant'. With your feet spread a bit, you squat quickly, then use your thigh muscles to shoot both you and the caber off the ground, and give the long spoke of the wheel the push that it needs to make a revolution.

6 If it falls back towards you, it is a '6 o'clock' – the best throw of all.

LONDON MOVIE LOCATIONS

London has provided the backdrop for hundreds of films. Here are just a few of the most recent movies shot in the capital.

Four Weddings And A Funeral (1993)
The smash-hit British movie starring Hugh Grant and Andie MacDowell takes in many locations, especially the chapel of the Royal Naval College, Greenwich, and Café Rouge in Wellington Street (the venue for the 'How many lovers?' conversation).

The Madness Of King George (1994)
The Oscar-winning movie starring Nigel Hawthorne was filmed at Syon House near Brentford, the Painted Hall of the Royal Naval College in Greenwich and inside St Paul's Cathedral.

101 Dalmatians (1996)
Locations for this live-action remake of the famous Disney cartoon include Trafalgar Square, Leicester Square, Burlington Arcade, Battersea Park and Kenwood House.

Lock, Stock And Two Smoking Barrels (1998)
Guy Ritchie's gangster movie was filmed at some of London's less salubrious locations – Borough Market, Bethnal Green Town Hall and Staples Market in Camden.

Shakespeare In Love (1998)
John Madden's period drama starring Gwyneth Paltrow and Joseph Fiennes, was filmed at Hatfield House, the Great Hall at Middle Temple, Marble Hill House, Spitalfields and St Bartholomew's church.

Notting Hill (1999)
Another smash-hit Brit flick starring Hugh Grant, this one was filmed a variety of locations in Notting Hill, plus Kenwood House, Nobu (restaurant), and the Savoy, Ritz and Hempel hotels.

The World Is Not Enough (1999)
The introductory scene of the James Bond movies is mainly filmed in London, at the MI6 building at Vauxhall Cross. The subsequent river chase takes in the Tate Gallery at Millbank, many famous London bridges and the Houses of Parliament. In typical style, Bond falls from a hot-air balloon on to the roof of the Millennium Dome.

THE POINT OF NO RETURN

Trafalgar Square, famous for Nelson's Column, is also the point from which London distances are measured, although the actual point is on the corner of the Strand and Charing Cross Road, near the statue of Charles 1. There is even a plaque on the wall to confirm this fact.

MUSEUMS FOR A VERY RAINY DAY

Corkscrew Museum, Alfriston, Sussex

Electric Shock Museum, Salcombe, Devon

Innoculation Museum, Berkeley, Gloucestershire

Lavatory Museum, Armitage, Staffordshire

Lawnmower Museum, Southport, Lancashire

Operating Theatre Museum, London

Pencil Museum, Keswick, Cumbria

Pilchard Museum, Newlyn, Penzance, Cornwall

Teapot Museum, Norwich Castle, Norfolk

LONDON'S TOP VISITOR ATTRACTIONS (PAID)

Attraction	Location	Visitors in 2002
British Airways London Eye	London	4,090,000
Tower of London	London	1,940,856
Westminster Abbey	London	1,058,854
Kew Gardens	London	969,188
London Zoo	London	891,028
Royal Academy of Arts	London	794,042
St Paul's Cathedral	London	781,364
Hampton Court Palace	Hampton Court	526,686
Buckingham Palace	London	334,654
Kensington Palace	London	307,672

THERE AIN'T HALF BEEN SOME CLEVER B******S

Britain has a deserved reputation as the home of some of the world's greatest inventors. Here are just ten, along with their ground-breaking inventions.

Inventor	Invented	Date
William Lee	Knitting machine	1589
John Napier	Logarithms	1614
Thomas Savery	Stream pump	1638
John Harrison	Chronometer (first portable and accurate timepiece)	1735
Thomas Saint	Sewing machine	1790
David Brewster	Kaleidoscope	1817
Charles Babbage	Automatic computer	1823
John Walker	Modern match	1827
Sir Frank Whittle	Jet engine	1930
Norman Rutherford and Michael Turner	Video Recorder	1957

VOLKS RAILWAY

The Volks Electric Railway, which runs eastwards from Brighton Pier, first opened in 1883 and is the oldest electric railway in Britain.

THE INVISIBLE BARRIER

Normally all that can be seen of the Thames Barrier are its nine stainless-steel piers. Under the water, however, are the 1,320-tonne (1,455-ton) gates that link each pier. In the event of a flood, the gates rotate 90 degrees until they are upright, forming a 20m- (66ft-) tall barrier. The Barrier was planned in 1971, work commenced in 1974, and it was officially opened in 1984.

WIZARD WINDMILL

The windmill at Bourn, Cambridgeshire, is a post mill – in other words, the whole structure revolves around a central support.

12 MONTHS OF SPORTING MADNESS

There is always some form of eccentric competitive craziness taking place somewhere in the UK. Here is a month-by-month guide to some of the oddest events.

January Mudathon, Maldon, Essex – a 180m (200yd) race through the freezing, waist-deep mud of the Blackwater River.

February Hurling The Silver Ball, Newquay, Cornwall – in which teams of 300 a side battle to hurl a silver ball through stone goalposts 3km (2 miles) apart.

March Whuppity Scourie, Lanark, Scotland – in which dozens of children run round a church hitting each other over the head with paper mallets before scrabbling for pennies thrown by local dignitaries.

April The World Coal Carrying Championship, Osset, West Yorkshire – in which burly men and women attempt to lug a 51kg (120lb) bag of coal uphill for 1.3km (4/5 mile).

May Cheese rolling, Gloucestershire – in which mostly drunken competitors chase huge cheeses down steep hills, usually breaking their legs in the process.

June World Toe Wrestling Championship, Ashbourne, Derbyshire – an annual battle of the big toes held at Ye Olde Royal Oak Inn, where the sport was invented more than 20 years ago.

July International Brick and Rolling Pin Championships, Stroud, Gloucestershire – just like it says on the tin: men compete to throw bricks, while their women lob rolling pins the furthest.

August Lawnmower Grand Prix 12-hour endurance race, Petworth, West Sussex – in which grown men race souped-up mowers around Brinsbury Agricultural College.

September Gurning Championships, Egremont, Cumbria – where prizes are awarded for the person able to pull the ugliest face; some competitors have their teeth removed especially for the occasion.

October World Conker Championships, Peterborough, Cambridgeshire – where saliva and sheep urine are just two of the substances used to harden up competitors' conkers.

November Biggest Liar In The World Contest, Holmrook, Cumbria – a chance for contestants from all over the country to tell whoppers and win big prizes.

December Uppies and Doonies, Kirkwall, Orkney Islands – a massive 200-a-side communal scrum that lasts four hours.

RABBIE BURNS AND THE MOUSE

The great Scottish poet Robert Burns was born on 25 January 1759 in a small thatched cottage on the family farm near Ayr, Scotland. He had minimal schooling, spending most of his days working on the farm, and it was while ploughing that he found a fieldmouse nest that he was about to destroy. This was the inspiration for his 'Ode Tae A Mouse [pronounced "moose"]'. Most people know the opening lines, 'Wee sleekit cowrin' timrous beestie, oh what a panic's in thy breestie', but fewer know that another line, 'The best laid schemes o' mice an' men gang aft a-gley', inspired John Steinbeck's *Of Mice And Men*!

Wee, sleekit, cowrin', tim'rous beastie,
O, what a panic's in thy breastie!
Thou need na start awa sae hasty,
Wi' bickering brattle!
I wad be laith to rin an' chase thee,
Wi' murd'ring pattle!

I'm truly sorry man's dominion,
Has broken Nature's social union,
An' justifies that ill opinion,
Which makes thee startle
At me, thy poor, earth-born companion,
An' fellow-mortal!

I doubt na, whiles, but thou may thieve;
What then? poor beastie, thou maun live!
A daimen icker in a thrave
'S a sma' request;
I'll get a blessin wi' the lave,
An' never miss't!

Thy wee-bit housie, too, in ruin!
It's silly wa's the win's are strewin!
An' naething, now, to big a new ane,
O' foggage green!
An' bleak December's winds ensuin,
Baith snell an' keen!

Thou saw the fields laid bare an' waste,
An' weary winter comin fast,
An' cozie here, beneath the blast,
Thou thought to dwell —

Till crash! the cruel coulter past
Out thro' thy cell.

That wee bit heap o' leaves an' stibble,
Has cost thee monie a weary nibble!
Now thou's turn'd out, for a' thy trouble,
But house or hald,
To thole the winter's sleety dribble,
An' cranreuch cauld!

But Mousie, thou art no thy lane,
In proving foresight may be vain;
The best laid schemes o' mice an' men
Gang aft a-gley,
An' lea'e us nought but grief an' pain,
For promis'd joy!

Still thou art blest, compar'd wi' me!
The present only toucheth thee:
But och! I backward cast my e'e,
On prospects drear!
An' forward, tho' I canna see,
I guess an' fear!

SPOOKS COME CLEAN

Once zealous about guarding their secrecy, MI6 came out of the closet big style in 1990, when they opened their new 'trifle' HQ at Vauxhall Bridge. The building was used in the opening sequence of the James Bond movie *Tomorrow Never Dies*.

NELSON WOULD NEVER BELIEVE IT – WHAT REALLY TOOK PLACE DURING THE CONSTRUCTION OF NELSON'S COLUMN IN TRAFALGAR SQUARE

Sir Edwin Landseer, sculptor of the lions from 1859 to 1866, was almost always drunk – as, indeed, were most of the workmen. For this reason, construction took 30 years, leading to mass protests. People stoned the lions when they were finally unveiled. Nelson's statue, weighing 18 tonnes (19 tons), had to be hauled up twice because the workers had made the crane 4m (14ft) too short. Or so it seemed. A subsequent investigation confirmed that, in fact, the column was 4m (14ft) too tall.

HOW TO ADDRESS ROYALTY

Next time you are writing to the Royal Family (well, doesn't everybody?), it is important that you address them properly.

The Queen

On the envelope: *To the Queen's Most Excellent Majesty*

Start the letter: *Madam* or *Your Majesty* or *May it please Your Majesty*

End the letter: *I have the honour to be Your Majesty's most obedient subject and servant*

The Duke of Edinburgh

On the envelope: *To His Royal Highness, The Duke of Edinburgh*

Start the letter: *Sir* or *Your Royal Highness*

End the letter: *I have the honour to be Your Royal Highness's most obedient servant*

The Prince of Wales

On the envelope: *To His Royal Highness, the Prince of Wales*

Start the letter: *Sir* or *Your Royal Highness*

End the letter: *I have the honour to be Your Royal Highness's most obedient servant*

Royal princes and dukes

On the envelope: *To His Royal Highness, the Prince...* or *To His Royal Highness, the Duke of...*

Start the letter: *Sir* or *Your Royal Highness*

End the letter: *I have the honour to be Your Royal Highness's most obedient servant*

Royal princesses and duchesses

On the envelope: *To Her Royal Highness, the Princess...* or *To Her Royal Highness, the Duchess of...*

Start the letter: *I have the honour to be Your Royal Highness's most obedient servant*

End the letter: *I have the honour to be Your Royal Highness's most obedient servant*

Dukes and duchesses

On the envelope: *To His Grace, the Duke of...* or *Her Grace the Duchess of...*

Start the letter: *Sir* or *Madam*; *My Lord Duke* or *Your Grace* (*Your Grace* will serve both)

End the letter: *I have the honour to be Your Grace's most obedient servant*

ALL WIGHT

The entire population of the world could stand on the Isle of Wight.

MUNRO BAGGING

Munros are mountains with heights above 914m (3,000ft). The original list was compiled by the slightly tragic figure of Sir Hector Munro, an early leader of mountaineering in Scotland. He compiled the first catalogue of all the hills higher than 914m (3,000ft) and came up with the rather larger than expected number of 280 or so. Munro then set out to climb them all, and intended to climb his last one in the summer of 1914, but he died on the Western Front before he could return.

Here, in ascending order, are the top 34 mountains for Munro baggers.

Height in m (ft)	Mountain
1,148 (3,766)	Ben Alder
1,150 (3,773)	Bidean nam Bian
1,150 (3,773)	Sgurr na Lapaich
1,151 (3,776)	Sgurr nan Ceathreamhnan
1,155 (3,789)	Derry Cairngorm
1,155 (3,789)	Lochnagar Cac Carn Beag
1,157 (3,796)	Beinn Bhrotain
1,165 (3,822)	Stob Binnein
1,171 (3,842)	Ben Avon Leabaidh an Daimh Bhuidhe
1,174 (3,852)	Ben More
1,177 (3,862)	Stob Choire Claurigh
1,181 (3,875)	Mam Sodhail
1,182 (3,878)	Beinn Mheadhoin
1,183 (3,881)	Carn Eige
1,197 (3,927)	Beinn a'Bhuird North Top
1,214 (3,983)	Ben Lawers
1,220 (4,003)	Carn Mor Dearg
1,221 (4,006)	Aonach Mor
1,234 (4,049)	Aonach Beag
1,245 (4,085)	Cairn Gorm
1,258 (4,127)	Sgor an Lochain Uaine
1,291 (4,236)	Cairn Toul
1,296 (4,252)	Braeriach
1,309 (4,295)	Ben Macdui
1,344 (4,409)	Ben Nevis

CANARY WHARF

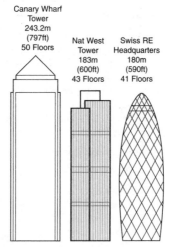

The Canary Wharf office complex rose from London's run-down docklands to become one of the jewels in the city's crown. Its centrepiece is the tower. Designed by Caesar Pelli, the 50-storey tower is 244m (800ft) tall – the tallest in Britain and the second tallest in Europe. It is clad in stainless steel around a framework constructed from 16,000 steel pieces weighing 27,430 tonnes (30,240 tons). It is built on a massive concrete raft that is supported by 212 deep piles.

WE SHALL REMEMBER THEM: THE CENOTAPH CEREMONY

The Cenotaph Ceremony is an unique expression of national homage, devoted primarily to remembrance of the dead of the two world wars. It is attended by the Sovereign and all the principal representatives of Parliament, the governments of the Commonwealth, the Armed Forces and the Churches. The Ceremony takes the form of a short Service of Dedication preceded by observation of the Two Minutes' Silence and official wreath laying. For this purpose the Cenotaph is enclosed in a square formed by detachments from branches of the Fighting Services, by a contingent from civilian services vital in time of war and by a large body of ex-Service men and women. The general public is invited to take part in the Service, and the Ceremony is broadcast in sound and television.

IT'S NOT JUST JELLIED EELS, YOU KNOW

Cosmopolitan London restaurants offer 70 different cuisines, including:

Africa – Ethiopian, Eritrean, Algerian, Sudanese, Nigerian, Tanzanian

Asian – Indian, Pakistani, Bangladeshi, Sri Lankan, Nepalese, Afghan

Caribbean – Jamaican, Guyanan

Chinese – Sichuan, Cantonese, Beijing

Classic British

European – Austrian, Swiss, German, Czech, Georgian, Hungarian, Polish, Russian, French, Italian, Belgian, Portuguese, Swedish, Danish, Spanish

Latin America – Argentinian, Brazilian, Colombian, Cuban, Peruvian

Middle Eastern – Moroccan, Lebanese, Tunisian, Egyptian

Modern British

North America – Tex-Mex, Mexican

Oriental – Japanese, Thai, Cambodian, Korean, Malaysian, Indonesian, Mongolian

Other cuisines – Burmese, Irish, Montenegrin, South African, Tibetan, Australian, New Zealand, Jewish

THE WITCHFINDER OF ESSEX

Matthew Hopkins, known as the Witchfinder General, was one of the most notorious figures to emerge from the 17th century. His headquarters were in Colchester, and in two years (from 1644) he was responsible for the deaths of at least 300 people, all supposedly witches. Manningtree also has quite a gruesome history, as many of Hopkins' victims were hanged on the diminutive village green.

GREAT FIRE, LUCKY ESCAPE

On 2 September 1666, a fire broke out in a baker's shop in Pudding Lane close to the site of St Paul's Cathedral. It quickly spread, destroying 87 churches, 44 livery halls and more than 13,000 houses. Remarkably, the Great Fire of London claimed just six lives.

LONG JOURNEY: THE TEN CITIES FURTHEST BY AIR FROM THE UK

Auckland	18,350km (11,400 miles)
Sydney	17,050km (10,600 miles)
Brisbane	16,550km (10,300 miles)
Perth	14,450km (9,000 miles)
Darwin	13,850km (8,600 miles)
Honolulu	11,600km (7,200 miles)
Singapore	10,950km (6,800 miles)
Kuala Lumpur	10,600km (6,600 miles)
Mauritius	9,800km (6,100 miles)
Hong Kong	9,650km (6,000 miles)

OFFICIAL FLYING OF THE UNION FLAG

February
6th – Queen's accession • *19th* – Prince Andrew's birthday

March
1st – St David's Day [Wales] • *10th* – Prince Edward's birthday •
2nd Monday – Commonwealth Day

April
21st – Queen's birthday • *23rd* – St George's Day [England]

May
9th – Europe Day

June
2nd – Coronation Day • *10th* – Duke of Edinburgh's birthday •
Varies – Queen's Official Birthday

August
15th – Princess Anne's birthday

November
Nearest Sunday to 11th – Remembrance Sunday •
14th – Prince of Wales' birthday • *20th* – Queen's Wedding Day •
30th – St Andrew's Day (Scotland)

CITY POPULATIONS

In descending order…

1.	London	7,926,000
2.	Birmingham	2,360,000
3.	Manchester	2,337,000
4.	Glasgow	1,648,000
5.	Leeds	1,580,000
6.	Newcastle	797,000
7.	Liverpool	690,000
8.	Sheffield	673,000
9.	Nottingham	631,000
10.	Bristol	568,000
11.	Edinburgh	527,000
12.	Belfast	437,000
13.	Cardiff	326,000

IMAGINE! IT'S JOHN LENNON'S HOUSE

'Imagine no possessions…' sang John Lennon in his famous hit song in 1970. The edge is taken off this sentiment if one considers that it was written and produced at his mansion in Tittenhurst Park Estate, Sunningdale, a house that boasts seven bedrooms, a swimming pool and 20 hectares (50 acres) of ground. When Lennon and Yoko Ono left for the US in 1971, the house was bought by former Beatles drummer Ringo Starr for £2 million ($3.3 million). He later sold it to Sheikh Zayed bin Sultan al-Nahyan of Abu Dhabi.

SOME FINGER-LICKING CULINARY STATISTICS

Eating out by visitors to London generates £1.6 billion ($2.7 billion) for the London economy.

The number of restaurant meals served per year in Britain in the last 17 years has grown from 338 million to 470 million.

The number of hotel meals served per year in Britain in the last 17 years has grown from 434 million to 640 million.

Pub meals have more than doubled since 1981 – from 670 million meals per year served to 1.4 billion.

HERE IN MY PLANE

The otherwise unremarkable A3051 Botley to Winchester road in Hampshire gained brief notoriety in January 1982, when electro-pop guru Gary Numan was forced to make a crash landing in his Cessna 210 plane. He narrowly missed a petrol lorry and a house.

DOGGETT'S COAT AND BADGE

Thomas Doggett was an 18th-century actor and comedian who was also manager of the Drury Lane theatre. Impressed by the skill of the watermen who plied their trade up and down the Thames (much like modern-day taxi drivers), and especially the way they dealt with the river's strong current, he inaugurated a race for them. The six selected rowers had to race, against the current, from Old Swan Pier at London Bridge to the Old White Swan Inn in Chelsea, for a distance of 7.2km (4.5 miles). The winner received a silver badge and red livery, which subsequently gave the race its name: Doggett's Coat and Badge. The race, first competed in 1715, is still run today and is the oldest boat race in Britain.

ROCK WITH THE CAVEMAN

Chislehurst Caves in Kent are a 32km- (20 mile-) long system of tunnels left behind after extensive chalk and flint mining. In the 1960s and 1970s, they became an unlikely rock venue when fans went underground to see the likes of Pink Floyd, Led Zeppelin and Jimi Hendrix perform.

TOP O' THE HILL

Royal Doulton's Top o' the Hill figurine was first produced in 1937, and is still sold today. The first range of figurines was produced in 1913, and in the intervening 90 years about 4,000 designs have been added.

OXFORD BAGS

William Richard Morris (1877–1963) started off as a bicycle repairer in 1893 at Cowley St John, near Oxford. In 1901, he went into the business of motorcycles, and subsequently built the first Morris 'Oxford' in 1913.

CANTERBURY TALE

Canterbury is Kent's most-visited tourist attraction, with more than two million visitors each year.

WREN'S REJECTS

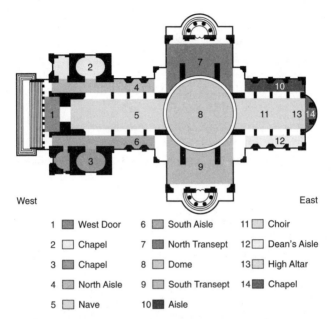

1	West Door	6	South Aisle	11	Choir
2	Chapel	7	North Transept	12	Dean's Aisle
3	Chapel	8	Dome	13	High Altar
4	North Aisle	9	South Transept	14	Chapel
5	Nave	10	Aisle		

Sir Christopher Wren's early designs for St Paul's Cathedral were rejected for being too revolutionary. He still managed to build Britain's only domed cathedral, although there are actually two smaller domes contained within the main outer structure. Wren's tomb, situated inside the cathedral, bears a Latin inscription which (translated) means, 'Reader, if you seek his monument, look around you.'

COCKNEY: AN EXPLANATION

The word 'cockney', traditionally used to describe a Londoner born within the sound of Bow Bells, derives from an earlier spelling, 'cokeney', which literally means 'cock's egg', a small malformed egg occasionally laid by young hens. During the 1700s the term, used by country folk, was applied to townsfolk who were considered ignorant of the established customs and country ways. This term in due course became synonymous with working-class Londoners themselves and has now lost its once-denigrating qualities. Despite the current definition of a cockney, to most outsiders a cockney is anyone from London itself.

SOME ESSEX GIRL JOKES

In the 1980s, girls from Essex won an unenviable reputation for being sex-crazed bimbos. Consequently, Essex Girl jokes are now as much a part of British culture as mother-in-law jokes. Here are a few of the cleaner ones.

How do you make an Essex girl laugh on a Saturday?
Tell her a joke on a Wednesday.

Why do Essex girls wear hoop earrings?
So they'll have somewhere to rest their ankles.

What do you call an Essex girl with half a brain?
Gifted!

What are the first three things an Essex girl does in the morning?
1 Says, 'Thanks, guys…'
2 Introduces herself.
3 Goes home.

Why did the Essex girl stop using the pill?
It kept falling out.

What do Essex girls do for foreplay?
Remove their underwear.

How did the Essex girl break her leg raking leaves?
She fell out of the tree.

Two Essex girls out walking in the country come upon some tracks. A furious argument ensues, with one of them saying they are badger tracks and the other insisting that they're deer tracks. They are still fighting when the train hits them.

SOUTHEAST RECORD BREAKERS

Largest Roman palace: Fishbourne, Sussex

Tallest Roman remain: The Pharos, Dover – 12m (40ft)

Largest castle: Dover Castle – 14 hectares (34 acres)

Oldest town: Colchester – founded AD 10

Oldest school: Kings, Canterbury – founded AD 600

Largest private house: Knole House, Kent – 365 rooms

Oldest house: Eastry Court, Kent – AD 603

LONDON'S TOP VISITOR ATTRACTIONS (FREE)

Attraction	Location	Visitors in 2002
Tate Modern	London	4,618,632
British Museum	London	4,607,311
National Gallery	London	4,130,973
Natural History Museum	London	2,957,501
Victoria and Albert Museum	London	2,661,338
Science Museum	London	2,628,374
National Portrait Gallery	London	1,484,331
Tate Britain	London	1,178,235
Somerset House	London	900,000 (estimate)
St Martin-in-the-Fields	London	700,000 (estimate)

CAB!

London first had horse-drawn buses in 1825. New York followed six years later. The first Hansom cabs (with driver sitting on a high seat at the rear) appeared in London in 1834.

TOP 10 POLICE FORCES WITH THE MOST SPEEDING CAMERAS

1. Metropolitan
2. Thames Valley
3. West Midlands
4. Staffordshire
5. Lancashire
6. Greater Manchester
7. West Yorkshire
8. South Yorkshire
9. South Wales
10. Essex

TOP 10 MUSEUMS AND GALLERIES

British Museum

National Gallery

Tate Gallery

Natural History Museum

Royal Academy

Science Museum

Glasgow Art Gallery

Victoria and Albert Museum

Burrell Collection

Jorvik Centre

A SELECTION OF HAUNTED HOTELS AND INNS

The Busby Stoop Inn

Location: Sand Hutton, North Yorkshire

Origin: 18th century

Story: Executed for murder in 1702, local drunkard and thief Thomas Busby's remains were hung from a gibbet – or stoop – opposite his favourite inn. Busby's ghost still haunts the gibbet, while a chair supposedly used by Busby was thought to have dire consequences for anyone who sat in it. It was later removed and can be seen in Thirsk Museum.

Falcon Hotel

Location: Castle Ashby, Northamptonshire

Origin: 17th century

Story: During the English Civil War, part of this hotel was a blacksmith's forge. Arthur was the blacksmith in the village, who loyally stood by his Royalist liege, the Marquis of Northampton. When passing Roundheads demanded that he reshoe their horses, Arthur refused – and was hanged from a walnut tree. He still haunts the garden, and occasionally helps himself to a drink from behind the bar.

The Old Ferryboat Inn

Location: Holywell, nr St Ives, Cambridgeshire

Origin: 1050

Story: The inn was built in Anglo-Saxon times. Its records show that liquor was served as early as AD 560. There is a slab in the floor of the inn which marks the burial place of 17-year-old Juliette Tewsley, who hanged herself after being turned down by the local woodcutter. She was buried in the pub because suicide victims were not allowed to be buried on consecrated ground. Juliette returns there on the anniversary of her death, to search for her lost love.

Scole Inn
Location: nr Diss, Norfolk
Origin: 18th century
Story: Emma, the wife of the landlord, was having an affair with a passing highwayman – or so her husband thought. In fact she was innocent, but the jealous pub owner murdered her anyway. She now haunts the pub and is known as the White Lady.

Weston Manor Hotel
Location: Weston-on-the-Green, Oxfordshire
Origin: 11th/12th century
Story: In the 11th century, this pub was a monastery. The monks who ran it were not terribly strict about their vows, and used to enjoy the company of a young local nun called Sister Maude. One day she was caught in *flagrante delicto* with one of the monks and was burned at the stake. She still haunts the pub to this day – especially one of the bedrooms, where it is thought she was caught doing the dirty deed.

The White Swan
Location: Harborne, near Birmingham
Origin: 19th century
Story: The pub dates back to 1714, but in the mid-19th century it was being used by local businessman John Wentworth as the venue for an illicit affair with a local girl. One day, while waiting for her in the pub, he was told about an accident outside. A wagon had overturned on the steep hill, and when they lifted it up they discovered Wentworth's lover crushed underneath. Devastated, he killed his loyal dog and then himself. His ghost still haunts the pub, wailing for the return of his dearly departed.

WHOLE LOTTA SHAKIN GOING ON

The Westbury Hotel in Conduit Street had just opened in 1958 when it received some publicity it surely could have done without. Among its guests in May that year was US rock 'n' roller Jerry Lee Lewis, accompanied by what he claimed to be his 13-year-old cousin Myra. Unfortunately for 'The Killer', newspaper hacks discovered that Myra was actually his wife. There was an outrage, which resulted in Jerry Lee cancelling his first UK tour and heading back across the Atlantic to face the music.

A BRIEF TOUR OF KEW GARDENS

Kew Gardens was created in 1759, for Princess Augusta, wife of Frederick, Prince of Wales.

Covering more than 288 acres, the Gardens contain around 25,000 different plant species, including 3,000 kept in the famous conservatories.

Two of the conservatories were designed by Decimus Burton. The larger Temperate House was, until the construction of the Eden Project's biomes, one of the largest glasshouses in Britain.

The Pagoda was built in 1761 and, at 50m (163ft), is the tallest pagoda in Britain.

Kew Gardens' conservatories include the oldest pot plant in the world – a single cycad called *Encephalatos altensteinii*, imported from South Africa in 1775 and still growing today.

ETON WALL GAME

It is not known exactly when the Eton Wall Game was first played, but the first recorded game was in 1766. The rules have been revised from time to time since 1849, but the game has remained essentially the same.

The field of play is a fairly narrow strip, about 5m (16ft) wide, running alongside a not-quite-straight brick wall, built in 1717 and about 110m (120yd) from end to end. Each side tries to get the ball down to the far end and then score. Players are not allowed to handle the ball and not allowed to let any part of their bodies except feet and hands touch the ground. They are also not allowed to strike or hold their opponents, and there are exceedingly strict 'offside' rules (no passing back and no playing in front). Apart from that, almost anything goes.

Each phase of play starts with a 'bully', when about six of the ten players from each side form up against the wall and against each other. Then the ball is rolled in and battle is joined. The player in possession of the ball will normally be on all fours, with the ball at his feet or under his knees. Players on his own side will attempt to support him, and to establish themselves in a position where he can pass the ball to them, or to disrupt the opposition. Likewise, players on the other side will attempt to obstruct his progress, to force him down, to gain possession of the ball themselves. Occasionally the ball becomes 'loose' and a player may be able to kick it out of play. The next bully is then formed opposite where the ball stops or is stopped (quite unlike what happens in soccer or rugby).

At each end of the wall is a special area known as 'calx'. When play reaches this area, the rules alter slightly (passing back becomes legal, for example) and the attacking side can score. The attackers try to raise the ball off the ground and against the wall – and, having done so, try to touch it with the hand. They then shout, 'Got it!' and if the umpire is satisfied that all is correct he shouts, 'Shy!' and awards them a 'shy', which is worth one point. The attackers can now attempt to throw a 'goal', which will bring them an extra nine points (the goals are a garden door at one end and a tree at the other). Shies are relatively common, perhaps half a dozen a year, but goals are very uncommon — the last one was in 1909, on St Andrew's Day.

IT'S YOUR FUNERAL

About 20 UK burials a year take place at sea.

TOP 10 GARDENS

Kew Gardens

Royal Botanic Gardens

Walsall Arboretum

Oxford University Botanic Gardens

Alnwick Castle Gardens

Belfast Botanic Gardens

Glasgow Botanic Gardens

Dixon Park, Belfast

Stourhead

Bodnant Gardens, North Wales

PINEWOOD, MR BOND

Pinewood Studios is the home of the largest studio sound stage. It was built especially for the 1976 James Bond movie *The Spy Who Loved Me*, and measures 103m by 42m by 12m (336ft by 139ft by 41ft). During filming, it was used to hold 5.6 million litres (1.5 million gallons) of water and full-scale sections of a 610-tonne (670,000-ton) oil tanker, as well as three full-size nuclear submarines.

THE BEST THEME-PARK RIDES IN BRITAIN

Air
Alton Towers
This is a new rollercoaster, which opened at the start of 2002. It travels at speeds of up to 70kph (44mph) and differs from most rollercoasters in that you are held parallel to the track.

Nemesis
Alton Towers
The legendary suspended coaster features forces up to 4G and speeds of up to 80kph (50mph).

Rip Saw
Alton Towers
Takes you 15m (50ft) up in the air, spins you around, looping and turning, and dangles you upside down into jets of water.

Oblivion
Alton Towers
Menacing-looking vertical-drop coaster. It features a 60m (197ft) drop, and reaches 110kph (69mph) with up to 4.5Gs.

Maelstrom
Drayton Manor, Tamworth
A stomach-churning, new gyro-swing. 32 riders sit in a circle with over-the-shoulder restraints, facing outwards for a better view. The circular gondola at the end of a 17.4m- (57ft-) long pendulum then swings into action – to a height of 22.5m (74ft) at an angle of 95 to 120 degrees – while simultaneously whirling and revolving.

Shockwave
Drayton Manor, Tamworth
Europe's only stand-up coaster. This is not for the faint-hearted.

Grand National
Blackpool Pleasure Beach
A big dipper but with lots of smaller dips, this has two trains on separate tracks that are 'racing' to the end.

The Pepsi Max Big One
Blackpool Pleasure Beach
At one time, this was the tallest roller coaster in the world. It's certainly an experience: the big drop just after it's finished climbing is made more intense by the fact that it turns, as well as being very steep.

Valhalla

Blackpool Pleasure Beach

A new ride that has quite a mixture of features, including fire, wind and water.

Samurai

Chessington World of Adventures

Six arms come out from a central axis, each containing five seats. The arms rotate on two axes and the whole assembly is attached to another arm. This raises it high in the air and also rotates, so just about every angle is covered. Halfway through the ride, the big arm slows down and then starts rotating the other way, to create yet another (different) range of sensations.

Colossus

Thorpe Park, Surrey

The world's first ten-looping roller coaster, featuring some slow 0G rolls that make you feel as if you're falling out.

X: No Way Out

Thorpe Park, Surrey

This is a roller coaster in the dark, but with a difference – it runs backwards!

Zodiac

Thorpe Park, Surrey

This carousel spins around fast and then turns you upside down. Similar to Enterprise at Alton Towers.

Quantum

Thorpe Park, Surrey

Similar to a magic-carpet-type ride, this is very fast – the platform is suspended at both sides and launches rapidly into the air, forwards and down again. Halfway through, it reverses, sending you the other way.

Hydro

Oakwood, Pembrokeshire

Europe's fastest and wettest water coaster, this has a near-vertical drop.

A HISTORIC PINT

The Dove pub, on the riverbank at Hammersmith, London, was once the favoured haunt of Charles II and Nell Gwynn. James Thompson composed 'Rule Britannia' in the bar.

SCOTT'S SLIMBRIDGE

Set up by Sir Peter Scott in 1946, Slimbridge is the world's largest and most varied wildfowl centre, with more than 4,000 birds representing 164 different species. The collection includes 400 flamingos.

THE TAY BRIDGE DISASTER

At approximately 7:15pm on the stormy night of 28 December 1879, the central navigation spans of the Tay Bridge collapsed into the Firth of Tay at Dundee, taking with them a train, six carriages and 75 souls to their fate. At the time, a gale estimated at force 10 to 11 was blowing down the Tay estuary at right angles to the bridge. The collapse of the bridge – which had only been open 19 months and was passed safe by the Board of Trade – sent shock waves through both the Victorian engineering profession and general public. The disaster is one of the most famous bridge failures and to date it is still the worst structural engineering failure in the British Isles.

What was perhaps worse was the poem subsequently composed about the disaster by William McGonagall:

The Tay Bridge Disaster
Beautiful Railway Bridge of the Silv'ry Tay!
Alas, I am very sorry to say
That ninety lives have been taken away
On the last Sabbath day of 1879,
Which will be remember'd for a very long time.

'Twas about seven o'clock at night,
And the wind it blew with all its might,
And the rain came pouring down,
And the dark clouds seem'd to frown,
And the Demon of the air seem'd to say,z
'I'll blow down the Bridge of Tay.'

MERSEY TUNNEL

4.6km (2.9 miles) long

254,000kg (560,000lb) explosives used to clear 910,000kg (1.3 million tons) of rock and clay

34 million litres (9 million gallons) of water pumped from the workings

1 million bolts used to hold its cast iron lining in place.

PHONE HOME?

More than 35 million people have telephones, whereas more than 50 million own mobile phones.

RIPON'S CLAIM TO FAME

The quiet Yorkshire market town is in fact, by dint of its cathedral, the oldest city in Britain. Its charter was awarded by Alfred the Great, in 886 – the first to be granted. London didn't receive its charter until 1066, while York's didn't arrive until 1396.

RAPID RAIL LINK

Britain's fastest ever passenger rail service was officially opened on 16 September 2003, when Eurostar trains ran at 298kph (186mph) on the Channel Tunnel Rail Link. The £1.9 billion ($3.2 billion) first section stretches 74km (46 miles) from Folkestone to Fawkham Junction in north Kent. The next section is due to open in 2007.

THE SOUTHEAST'S TOP VISITOR ATTRACTIONS (PAID)

Attraction	Location	Visitors in 2002
Colchester Zoo	Stanway	504,406
Whipsnade Wild Animal Park	Dunstable	456,896
Woburn Safari Park	Woburn	415,787
Imperial War Museum, Duxford	Cambridge	382,255
Southend-On-Sea Pier	Southend-on-Sea	374,299
Paradise Wildlife Park	Broxbourne	Around 260,000
King's College Chapel	Cambridge	212,244
Banham Zoo	Banham	201,724
Sutton Hoo Burial Site	Sutton Hoo	198,000
Activity World	Hatfield	Around 170,000

LONDON EYE-POPPING FACTS

Opened to celebrate the Millennium, the London Eye has become a landmark on the south bank of the Thames, opposite the Houses of Parliament. The passenger capsules of the Eye incorporate an entirely new design form for observation wheels. Instead of being suspended under gravity, they turn within circular mounting rings fixed to the outside of the main rim, thereby allowing a spectacular 360-degree panorama at the top. Amazing facts about the London Eye include the following:

Its total power requirement is 500Kw – equal to six lightbulbs per person if the wheel is at full capacity.

The 32 capsules can carry 15,000 visitors a day.

It took over a week to lift the wheel vertical from a horizontal position across the Thames. This kind of procedure had previously only been attempted in oil-rigging operations.

The wheel will turn continuously, at an average of 8,000 times every year.

Passengers can see more than 40km (25 miles) in every direction, offering aerial views of some of the most famous sights, including St Paul's Cathedral, the Palace of Westminster and Windsor Castle.

The Wheel is London's fifth tallest structure, behind Canary Wharf, the Nat West Tower, the London Gherkin and the Telecom Tower. It is over 35m (115ft) taller than Big Ben, nearly 30m (98ft) taller than St Paul's Cathedral and almost three times as high as the Statue of Liberty.

At 135m (443ft) tall, the Eye is over twice the height of the famous Prater Wheel in Vienna – seen in the classic film *The Third Man* – and outstrips by 30m (98ft) the previous tallest observation wheel in Yokohama Bay, Japan.

ENGLISH MONARCHS

Svein Forkbeard	1014
Canute	1017–35
Harald Harefoot	1035–40
Hardicanute	1040–42
Edward the Confessor	1042–66
Harold II	1066
William the Conqueror	1066–87
William Rufus	1087–1100
Henry I	1100–35
Stephen	1135–54

Henry II	1154–89
Richard the Lionheart	1189–99
John	1199–1216
Henry III	1216–72
Edward I	1272–1307
Edward II	1307–27
Edward III	1327–77
Richard II	1377–99
Henry IV	1399–1413
Henry V	1413–22
Henry VI	1422–61, 1470–71
Edward IV	1461–70, 1471–83
Edward V	1483
Richard III	1483–85
Henry VII	1485–1509
Henry VIII	1509–47
Edward VI	1547–53
Lady Jane Grey	1553 (nine days)
Mary Tudor	1553–8
Elizabeth I	1558–1603
James I	1603–25
Charles I	1625–49
[Oliver Cromwell	1649–58
Richard Cromwell]	1658–59
Charles II	1660–85
James II	1685–88
William III	1689–1702
Anne	1702–14
George I	1714–27
George II	1727–60
George III	1760–1820
George IV	1820–30
William IV	1830–37
Victoria	1837–1901
Edward VII	1901–10
George V	1910–36
Edward VIII	1936
George VI	1936–52
Elizabeth II	1952–present

GRETNA GREEN

Gretna Green, in southern Scotland, is one of the world's most famous wedding venues, conjuring up stories of romance, scandals and illicit trysts. For 250 years, thousands of young lovers have made for the village, which lies just over the English border, where they can wed in a hurry under Scotland's lenient marriage laws. Countless stories recall lovers arriving in Gretna Green after days on the road, with an angry father in hot pursuit, keen to intercept the couple before the marriage can take place. No place in the world can claim such a rich wedding history – indeed, one of the oldest marriage certificates is dated 11 June 1772. The rush to Gretna Green continues to this day. Over 4,000 couples marry there annually, accounting for about 13 per cent of all weddings performed in Scotland.

UGH! TRADITIONAL HAGGIS INGREDIENTS

1 calf's kidney

1 calf's udder

1 calf's pluck*

1 bay leaf

12 sprigs of parsley

1 handful of young green onions

1 handful of shallots

1 handful of small mushrooms

1 tablespoon of butter

1 wineglass of Madeira wine

salt and pepper

web of veal fat

2 tablespoons of gravy

egg yolks

1 handful of brown breadcrumbs

heart, liver, lungs

When a parcel containing haggis was flown to Brazil in 1965, customs officers decided that they couldn't decide what it was. It was analysed and declared to be a fertiliser.

DYB DYBING AT BROWNSEA

Brownsea Island in the middle of Poole Harbour became the site of the first ever Boy Scout camp, when, in 1907, Lord Baden Powell took 20 youngsters there for a week.

THE NEW FOREST

The New Forest was created by William the Conqueror as his own personal hunting park. There weren't many trees – mostly gorse and scrub – and local people were forbidden (on pain of death) from interfering with the land or the animals. It eventually became an important source of oak for shipbuilding.

BRITAIN'S LONGEST RIVERS

Severn	354km (220miles)
Thames	346km (215 miles)
Tay	188km (117 miles)
Usk	104km (65 miles)

THE 'ELECTRIC BRAE'

The 'Electric Brae', known locally as Croy Brae, is a stretch of road that runs the 400m (1/4 mile) from the bend overlooking Croy railway viaduct in the west to the east. While there is this slope of 1:86 upwards from the bend at the Glen, the configuration of the land on either side of the road provides an optical illusion, making it look as if the slope is going the other way. Therefore, a stationary car on the road with the brakes off will appear to move slowly uphill. The term 'Electric Brae' dates from a time when it was incorrectly thought to be a phenomenon caused by electric or magnetic attraction within the brae, or hill.

DESIGNER RESORT

Southend-on-Sea was a designer resort created in the 18th century to attract day-trippers from London. It got its name because it was a purpose-built development at the south end of the village of Prittlewell.

OXBRIDGE – THE TRUTH

Oxford University was founded in 1167, by English students fleeing unrest in France.

Cambridge University was founded in 1209, by students fleeing from unrest at Oxford University.

SOME GREAT BRITISH HOBBIES

Catapulting

Enthusiasts stage regular competitions to see whose home-made catapult can fling them the furthest distance. This is not without danger, however: in 2000, Stella Young from London was catapulted at more than 80kph (50mph) into a net 90m (100yd) away, and fractured her pelvis when she bounced out.

Tree hugging

An increasingly popular hobby, hugging the nearest tree is a highly recommended stress-buster, according to Rod Nicholson of the Centre for Harmony in Gloucester. He claims that people who have tried it are more relaxed, they sleep better, and make better decisions at work. 'If we used it widely here, we could cut the NHS bill in half,' he says.

Drain spotting

If you see someone in an anorak staring down at a manhole cover, they are most likely to be a drain spotter. Enthusiasts make notes of the unique serial number of each metal cover, then trace it back to the year and origin of manufacture.

Self-burying

Some folk just like to get away from it all – by burying themselves 2m (6ft) underground. It seems rather a solitary hobby, but is popular nonetheless. In 1999, loner Geoff Smith of Mansfield, Nottinghamshire, spent 147 days buried in a specially constructed coffin in his garden. In the process, he won the world record title once held by his late mother Emma, who spent 100 days down a hole in Skegness, Lincolnshire, in 1968.

Naturism

According to the British Naturism Organisation, letting it all hang out is a 'friendly, relaxing and enjoyable way to spend your free time'. And you won't be alone with this hobby, with over 25,000 registered naturists in the UK and more than two million worldwide. The number of nudist beaches is increasing all the time, too – there are currently nine on the south coast of England alone.

Norbert Dentressangling

For years, Eddie Stobart-spotters have gathered on motorway bridges for a glimpse of the Cumbrian-based haulage firm's distinctive lorries. But a breakaway group of Euro trucking enthusiasts have now switched their attention to wagons belonging to Stobart's French rival, Norbert Dentressangle. Bryan Wiley, of 'Dentressanglers UK', says: 'They come from all over the continent and it's a thrill to compare notes with other spotters to see where they've been. The attraction is in the smart livery – and of course the unmistakable name.'

MOTHER-IN-LAW JOKES

As much a part of British culture as fish and chips and rainy summers, the poor old mother-in-law has provided the butt of the joke for generations of comedians. Here are just a few side-splitters:

Is it possible to kill a mother-in-law with newspaper?
Yes, if you wrap an iron in it.

I bought my mother-in-law a chair for Christmas – but she wouldn't plug it in.

What's the difference between a dead mother-in-law lying in the middle of the road, and a dead dog lying in the middle of the road? There are skidmarks in front of the dog!

I always know when it's the mother-in-law knocking at the door – the mice throw themselves in the traps.

The definition of mixed emotions: seeing your mother-in-law drive over the cliff in your new car.

'I took my dog to the vet today because it bit my mother-in-law.'
'Did you put it to sleep?'
'No – I had its teeth sharpened.'

ZIGGY'S PHONE BOX

The famous red telephone box featured on the cover of David Bowie's *Ziggy Stardust And The Spiders From Mars* album was originally situated in Heddon Street, London. It was replaced by an 'open-plan' metal and glass phone box in the late 1970s, but that has not stopped thousands of Bowie fans scrawling graffiti over the walls where the original phone box stood.

THE OLDEST PUB IN BRITAIN

Bottoms up to Ye Olde Fighting Cocks, in St Albans, which dates back to the 16th century.

THE GEOGRAPHICAL CENTRE OF BRITAIN

54.00°N, 2.00°W

THE PLACE FOR A GOOD READ

Foyle's bookshop on Charing Cross Road, in London, carries a stock of approximately six million books. These are displayed on 48km (30 miles) of shelving, spread over five floors.

THE SOUTHEAST'S TOP VISITOR ATTRACTIONS (FREE)

Attraction	Location	Visitors in 2002
Pleasure Beach	Great Yarmouth	Around 1,500,000
Norwich Cathedral	Norwich	Around 500,000
St Albans Cathedral	St Albans	Around 280,979
Mannings Amusement Park	Felixstowe	Around 270,000
Cambridge American Cemetery	Coton	Around 175,000
Norfolk Lavender	Heacham	Around 150,000
Southwold Pier	Southwold	Around 150,000
Thorndon Countryside Centre	Thorndon	Around 131,000

SHOPPING MANIA

The Lakeside Shopping Centre at Thurrock, Essex is the largest in the UK, boasting over 320 shops, four major department stores, 30 cafés and restaurants, a seven-screen multiplex cinema, a chapel and a 10.5-hectare (26-acre) lake complete with PADI-certified diving school complex. Lakeside has an average of 500,000 visitors per week and more than 160 million people have visited the shopping centre since it opened in October 1990. It enjoys parking for 13,000 cars and 250 coaches.

THE LOCH NESS MONSTER: FIRST SIGHTINGS

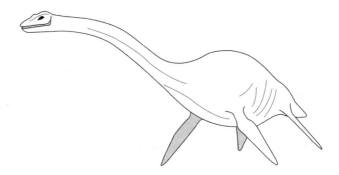

Loch Ness, the largest freshwater lake in the British Isles, is 38km (24 miles) long and, at one point, 2.5km (1¹/₂ miles) wide. It has an average depth of 137m (450ft) and at times plunges closer to 300m (1,000ft). It is cold and murky, with dangerous currents – in short, the perfect place to hide a monster from even the most prying eyes of science.

In AD 565, Loch Ness's story was written down. The account tells of St Columba, who saved a swimmer from the a hungry lake monster, and from then on rumours about the creature were repeated from time to time. In 1933, after a new road was built along the edge of the Loch, the number of reports soared. The first of this period came on 14 April, when the owners of an inn in Drumnadrochit observed an 'enormous animal…rolling and plunging' in the loch. They reported it to Alex Campbell, the man in charge of regulating salmon fishing in the loch. He spent a lot of time at the lake and observed the monster himself several times after being told of the sighting. Campbell described the creature as having 'a long, tapering neck, about 6 feet [2m] long, and a smallish head with a serpentine look about it, and a huge hump behind', and estimated the 'monster's' length to be about 30ft (over 9m).

In 1933, the first photograph was taken by Hugh Gray, who reported, 'I immediately got my camera ready and snapped the object which was then two to three feet [60cm to 90cm] above the surface of the water. I did not see any head, for what I took to be the front parts were under the water, but there was considerable movement from what seemed to be the tail.'

THE WEATHER: IT'S OFFICIAL

Britain has notoriously capricious weather. However, the official British climate is temperate, moderated by prevailing southwest winds over the North Atlantic Current, with more than half of the days overcast.

GOING UP?

Britain's first escalators were installed at Harrod's in 1889. An attendant was employed to stand at the top of the escalators, offering either brandy or smelling salts to any terrified customers.

BRITAIN'S BIGGEST CAR PARK

The M25 motorway encircles London, and forms the southern terminus of eight motorways (clockwise from the north): the M1, M11, M20, M26, M23, M3, M4 and M40. It is used by 170,000 vehicles a day, and has a well-deserved reputation for traffic jams. In a typical day in November 1996, for example, researchers estimated that the M25 caused around 518,000 motorists to waste the equivalent of 29 years of their lives.

SOME FASCINATING FACTS ABOUT BRIGHTON

8 million people visit the city-by-the-sea each year.

Brighton and Hove is one of the UK's top ten destinations for overseas visitors – 310,000 stay here each year.

The city attracts 200,000 conference delegates a year.

Brighton was voted in the top ten in the 2000 *Observer* Travel Award for Best UK City.

The Royal Pavilion attracts 350,000 visitors a year and was nominated 'best history and heritage attraction in Britain' by *Holiday Which?* magazine in 2002.

Brighton Pier is the UK's fourth most-visited leisure attraction.

THE REAL ST ANDREW

Andrew was a disciple of Jesus and the brother of Simon Peter. The two are pictured as fishermen working beside the sea when Jesus summons them to follow him and become 'fishers of men'. Although less prominent than his brother, Andrew is present at the miracle of the bread and the speech on the Mount of Olives. In the list of the Twelve, Andrew is listed second in Luke and Matthew, and fourth in the books of Mark and Acts. In all accounts he was one of the first, as a follower of John the Baptist, to be 'called' a disciple.

According to later traditions, Andrew became a missionary to Asia Minor, Macedonia and southern Russia. In AD 70 he was martyred in Patras, Greece – having many converts, he was feared by the Roman governor, who had him crucified on an X-shaped cross known as a Saltire Cross. And it is this cross-shape that is reflected in the Scottish flag. Andrew is the patron saint not only of Scotland, but also Greece and Russia. He is invoked against gout and a stiff neck!

BRITAIN'S TOURIST INDUSTRY

Research collected together by the British Tourist Authority shows that tourism is one of the largest industries in the UK, worth approximately £63.9 billion ($106 billion) in 1999.

The UK ranks fifth in the international tourism earnings league behind the USA, Italy, France and Spain.

The top four overseas markets for the UK in 1999 were the USA, France, Germany and Ireland.

There are an estimated 1.85 million jobs in tourism in the UK, accounting for around 7 per cent of all employed people in Great Britain. There are more jobs in tourism than in construction or transport.

COME FLY WITH ME

There are 470 airports in Britain, and 11 heliports.

THE DWINDLING EMPIRE

A century ago, a map of the world would have shown most of it painted in the red of the British Empire. Today, the empire has largely gone – although Britain does still have dependencies. None of them are quite the size of India, though:

Anguilla, Bermuda, British Indian Ocean Territory, British Virgin Islands, Cayman Islands, Falkland Islands, Gibraltar, Guernsey, Isle of Man, Jersey, Montserrat, Pitcairn Islands, St Helena, South Georgia and the South Sandwich Islands, Turks and Caicos Islands

ESSENTIAL FACTS ABOUT THE LONDON UNDERGROUND

Highest point: Amersham on the Metropolitan Line – 152.4m (500ft) above sea level

Highest point above the ground: Dollis Brook Viaduct on the Mill Hill East branch of the Northern Line – 18.3m (60ft) above the road below

Lowest point: south of Waterloo station on the Northern Line, where the tracks are 21.3m (70ft) below sea level

Absolute deepest part of the system: Northern Line, where (below Hampstead Heath) the rails are over 67.1m (220ft) below the ground.

Furthest places reached by London Underground trains: Epping (Central Line) in the north, Morden (Northern Line) in the south, Upminster (District Line) in the east and Amersham (Metropolitan Line) in the west

Longest continuous journey on the Underground (without a change of trains): Central Line, West Ruislip to Epping – 54.4km (34 miles)

Longest journey underground: Northern Line, Morden to East Finchley via the City branch – 27.2km (17 miles)

Longest distance between adjacent stations: Metropolitan Line, Chesham to Chalfont and Latimer – 6.4km (4 miles)

Shortest distance between adjacent stations: Piccadilly Line, Leicester Square to Covent Garden – 256m (0.16 miles)

Shortest line on the system: Waterloo and City Line – 2.2km (1.38 miles)

Busiest line: District Line – 180 million passengers per year over its 64km (40 mile) length

Busiest station: Victoria – 85 million passengers each year

Shortest escalator: Chancery Lane station, linking the eastbound and westbound platforms of the Central Line, which are immediately above each other

Longest escalator: Angel station on the City branch of the Northern Line

Biggest stations on the network: Baker Street and Moorgate (both ten platforms)

Smallest stations on the network: Heathrow Terminal 4, Chesham, Mill Hill East (one platform each)

UNLUCKY, SON

On Armistice Day (11 November) 1918, Able Seaman Richard Morgan of Gwent, Monmouthshire, died while serving on HMS *Garland*. He thus became the last British serviceman to die in World War I and the last of 40,000 Welshmen to lose their lives in the fighting.

CARDIFF'S SUPERSTADIUM

Completed in time for the World Rugby Cup competition held in Cardiff in 1999, the Millennium Stadium is one of the finest sporting arenas in the UK. The 75,000-seat, all-weather stadium replaced the world-famous Arms Park to become the world's largest arena with a retractable roof. It also contains a rugby museum, a riverside walk, a public plaza and is suitable for all sporting events and concerts.

USELESS FACTS ABOUT THE BRITISH

The weight of rubbish thrown out by the average Brit is 680kg (1,500lb).

51 per cent of Brits sleep naked.

Up to 14 million Brits say they can trace their ancestry back to Ireland.

73 per cent of British women buy their first home on their own.

The best place to find a partner is Scotland – 79 per cent of Scots claim to be in a relationship.

A sex-change operation has never been performed in Ireland.

17 per cent of Brits work more than 48 hours a week.

Less than 30 per cent of British women are happy with their bodies.

British workers travel 125 billion km (78.5 billion miles) a year just to get to work.

One in three Brits go on a foreign holiday every four months.

Only 45 per cent of working adults have a nine-to-five office job.

75 per cent of Brits are unhappy in their job.

70 per cent of British kids have access to the Internet.

ACCOMMODATION USED BY FOREIGN VISITORS TO THE UK

Accommodation type	%
Hotels	45
Bed and breakfast	5
Camping/mobile home	1
Hostel	4
Holiday village/centre	0
Rented house	3
Paying guest	3
Free guest	39
Own home	2
Other	5
Total bedspace	
England	1,029,875
Scotland	103,788
Wales	28,304
Northern Ireland	32,176
Total	**1,194,143**

BRITISH INDUSTRY

According to the *CIA Worldbook*, British industry produces 'machine tools, electric power equipment, automation equipment, railroad equipment, shipbuilding, aircraft, motor vehicles and parts, electronics and communications equipment, metals, chemicals, coal, petroleum, paper and paper products, food processing, textiles, clothing, and other consumer goods'.

MAGNIFICENT MARINA

Brighton's marina, which opened in 1978, is Europe's largest man-made marina and holds more than 2,000 boats.

SEVERN SUICIDES

A well-known suicide spot, the Severn Bridge Service Station, was where Richey Edwards' silver Vauxhall Cavalier was found in February 1995. It was 15 days since the Manic Street Preachers' guitarist had gone missing from a hotel in London, and he has never been seen since.

CHIPPENHAM'S TWIN CLAIMS TO FAME

This Wiltshire town is famous for two things: its market and Eddie Cochrane. It was here in 1960 that the 1950s rocker, famed for 'C'mon Everybody' and 'Three Steps To Heaven', was killed. The taxi Cochrane was travelling in skidded into a lamppost on the A4 at Rowden Hill. His fellow performer Gene Vincent was also in the crash, but he survived. Bizarrely, Cochrane's guitar was rescued from the scene by a rookie police officer called Dave Harmon (who would later become the Dave in 1960s popsters Dave Dee, Dozy, Beaky, Mick and Tich).

THE WEIRD WORLD OF GLASTONBURY

Glastonbury is said to be the site of the Isle of Avalon, the Celtic dreamworld where King Arthur was buried. It's also claimed that Joseph of Arimathea buried the Holy Grail under Glastonbury Tor and planted a staff that turned into a thorn tree which only flowers at Christmas. Whatever the truth, the area has continued to attract mystics, pagans and hippies throughout the centuries. Archaeologists suggest midsummer festivals took place in the area as far back as 500 BC, and in the 1920s George Bernard Shaw was behind an arts festival staged there. Local farmer Michael Eavis decided to put on a music festival at Glastonbury in 1970, and managed to book T-Rex and David Bowie. More than 1,500 people turned up, each paying £1 ($1.70). The following year, 7,000 music fans saw the likes of Hawkwind, Fairport Convention and Traffic, and the success of the Glastonbury Festival was established. Despite concerns about security – and hippies drowning in the mud – it now attracts top acts and crowds in excess of 100,000.

THE MOORS! READ ALL ABOUT THEM!

The southwest prong of England is dominated by three vast areas of moorland. The bleakness of Exmoor, Dartmoor and Bodmin Moor have inspired some of British literature's finest classic novels.

	Exmoor	Dartmoor	Bodmin Moor
Size	686 sq km (265 sq miles)	945 sq km (365 sq miles)	200 sq km (80 sq miles)
Highest point	Dunkery Beacon 517m (1,705ft)	High Willays 618m (2,038ft)	Brown Willy 417m (1375ft)
Novel	Lorna Doone (RD Blackmore)	The Hound Of The Baskervilles (Arthur Conan Doyle)	Jamaica Inn (Daphne du Maurier)

AN A–Z OF BRITISH-ISMS

and pigs might fly! Yeah, right!

aggro hassle, trouble

all mouth and no trousers boastful and without just reason

argy-bargy a heated argument

back of beyond middle of nowhere

bairn Scottish for 'baby'

barney argument

bobby-dazzler a amazing thing or person

Bob's your uncle There you go, That's all there is to it, Sorted!

boff fed up

bull in a china shop someone who acts before they think, without tact

cheesed off fed up

cake 'ole mouth (cakehole, eg Shut your cake 'ole)

chew the fat chat

chuck it down to rain, often heavily (eg It's going to chuck it down)

chucky-egg a boiled egg, or a pet name for partner, or young child

Corporation pop water (northern use)

daft as a brush stupid (eg You're as daft as a brush)

do a bunk/runner disappear, be on the run

Ey up! Hiya!

eyes are bigger than your belly think you can eat more than you can

Flaming Nora! an exclamation of anger or surprise

gaff home

gander look (eg Have a gander at that)

gearstick shiftstick in the US

Get your kit off! Get undressed!

give the elbow reject (eg I got the elbow, I was given the elbow)

Give it some wellie! Get some energy into it!

hollow legs refers to someone who could eat all day, and never fill up

how's your father sex (eg Fancy a bit of 'how's your father'?)

in good nick in good condition

jennel an alley

jumper sweater

keep your pecker up try to remain cheerful even if times are difficult

knockers breasts

life of Riley an easy life (eg He's got the life of Riley)

load of old cobblers a load of lies (i.e. what a load of old cobblers!)

Lord Muck The deprecatory name for a pompous conceited man (female equivalent: **Lady Muck**)

moaning Minnie a person who persistently grumbles

monkey one pound sterling (less well-known)
naff worthless, useless
not a full shilling stupid (refering to an old 5p coin, pre-decimalisation)
order of the boot to get lost (past tense, eg I gave him the order of the boot)
pop one's clogs die (eg He popped his clogs)
quid one pound sterling (£1)
rabbit/rattle talk a lot (eg Men tend to rattle just as much as women)
sound as a pound can't fault it
sweet Fanny Adams absolutely nothing
take the mickey (Mick/Michael) laugh at someone
talent an attractive person
thick as pudding stupid (ie referring to Yorkshire pudding)
thick as two short planks stupid (eg He is as thick as two short planks)
That takes the biscuit! That's the last straw!
throw a wobbly get very angry
umpteen many, a lot of (ie There were umpteen colours to choose from)
up the swanny in a hopeless situation, means the same as 'up the creek without a paddle'
veggie vegetarian
verbal diarrhoea incessant and aimless talk (eg He's got verbal diarrhoea)
wet one's whistle have a drink
work like a Trojan work very hard
yonks ages, for ever (eg It lasted for yonks)
zilch nothing (zero in US)

SOME FASCINATING FACTS ABOUT FARMING

British farmers produce enough beef and lamb for over 500 million Sunday roasts every year.

There are more free-range hens in the UK than anywhere else in Europe.

British farmers produce 39 litres (68 million pints) of fresh milk every day.

Every day, 9 million loaves of bread are baked in Britain.

The barley produced by British farmers helps make the 124 litres (218 pints) of beer and lager that the average person drinks in a year.

Every year, we eat 560 million bacon butties.

British growers produce over 100 different crops of fruit, vegetables, salad and herbs.

ISLAND LIFE

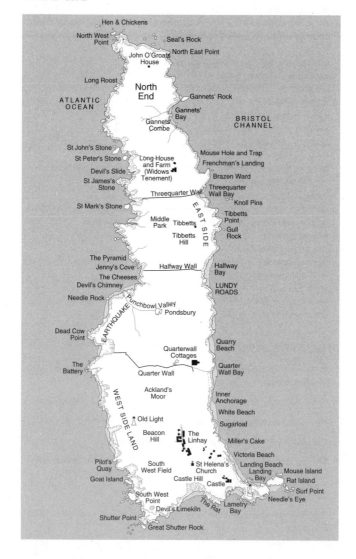

About 19km (12 miles) off the Devon peninsula sits Lundy Island, which is also known as Puffin Island due to its unusually high concentration of the brightly beaked birds. A mere 5km (3 miles) long by 1km ($3/8$ mile) wide, Lundy is also renowned as the haunt of such wildlife as ponies, deer and rabbits. Just be sure not to mix Lundy up with its near-neighbour, Rat Island – this tiny outcrop is, as the name suggests, the lair of thousands of wild black rats.

HE'S NOT A NUMBER – HE'S A FREE MAN!

When number 6 (Patrick McGoohan) awakes from a drug-induced coma in episode 1 of cult '60s TV show *The Prisoner*, he is amazed to find himself in 'The Village'. The effect is very much the same for visitors to the real-life Portmeirion today – after all, there aren't too many Italian-style villages in Wales. Portmeirion was the brainchild of designer Sir Clough Williams-Ellis, who first drew up blueprints in the 1920s and then spent the next 40 years piecing his dream together. Today, thanks mainly to the cult status it achieved in McGoohan's psychedelic series, it attracts nearly half a million visitors a year.

SHAKEY'S TOMB

Shakespeare's tombstone in Stratford's Holy Trinity Church bears this inscription, said to have been written by him: 'Good friend, for Jesus' sake forbear to dig the dust enclosed here. Blest be the man that spares these stones, and curst be he that moves my bones.'

THE UNION FLAG

The Union Flag has a blue background with the red cross of St George (patron saint of England) edged in white and superimposed on the diagonal red cross of St Patrick (patron saint of Ireland). This is, in turn, superimposed on the diagonal white cross of St Andrew (patron saint of Scotland). The design and colours (especially the Blue Ensign) have been the basis for a number of other flags, including dependencies, Commonwealth countries, and others.

The Union Flag does not include the Welsh flag, as Wales is a principality of England and therefore, technically, the English flag takes precedent. Also note that, while St George's flag of England and St Andrew's flag of Scotland are the official flags of the respective countries, the flag of St Patrick is not the official flag of Northern Ireland.

THE ROYAL DIGIT

Anne Boleyn, Queen Elizabeth I's mother, had six fingers on her left hand.

BLUE PLAQUES

The first official London plaques were erected in 1867 by the Royal Society of Arts at the instigation of William Ewart MP. By 1901, they had put up 36 plaques, the oldest of which now surviving are those that commemorate Napoleon III and the poet John Dryden (both erected in 1875). The responsibility for putting up the plaques passed on to the London County Council in 1901, and the total of plaques had been extended to 298 by the time the Greater London Council (GLC) took over in 1965. The official plaque scheme was extended further until the GLC was disbanded in 1985. The first plaque set up by English Heritage was erected in 1986, and since that date at least 12 have been put up by them each year. There are about 700 official plaques in total, and most of them are blue with white lettering. The most-visited plaques in London are:

SHERLOCK HOLMES
Fictional British consulting detective
221b Baker Street

JOHN F KENNEDY
(1917–63)
35th American president
14 Princes Gate

CHARLES DICKENS
(1812–70)
Novelist
48 Doughty Street

KARL MARX
(1818–83)
German social, economic and political theorist
28 Dean Street

JOHN LOGIE BAIRD
(1888–1946)
British (Scottish) engineer who invented television
22 Frith Street

BRITAIN'S RICHEST ROCK STARS

	Name	Worth (£/$)
1	Paul McCartney	760 million (1,278 million)
2	Mick Jagger	175 million (294 million)
3	Elton John	170 million (286 million)
4	Sting	165 million (277 million)
5	Keith Richards	150 million (252 million)
5*	Tom Jones	150 million (252 million)
7	David Bowie	120 million (200 million)
7*	Eric Clapton	120 million (200 million)
7*	Phil Collins	120 million (200 million)
10	Ringo Starr	115 million (193 million)
11	Roger Waters	100 million (168 million)
12	Barry and Robin Gibb	94 million (158 million)
13	Ozzy Osbourne	85 million (142 million)
14	Dave Gilmour	75 million (126 million)
14*	Engelbert Humperdinck	75 million (126 million)
16	Mark Knopfler	70 million (117 million)
16*	Charlie Watts	70 million (117 million)
18	Robbie Williams	68 million (114 million)
19	George Michael	60 million (100 million)
19*	Jimmy Page	60 million (100 million)
19*	Robert Plant	60 million (100 million)
19*	Rod Stewart	60 million (100 million)

CAERPHILLY DOES IT

During the Civil War, Oliver Cromwell's troops attempted to blow up Caerphilly Castle so that Royalist troops couldn't use it as a stronghold. Their explosives succeeded in undermining the foundations of the southeast tower but, unfortunately for them, this resulted only in the tower tilting. It still stands today, leaning at a greater angle than the Leaning Tower of Pisa.

THE SOUTHWEST'S TOP VISITOR ATTRACTIONS (PAID)

Attraction	Location	Visitors in 2002
Eden Project	St Austell	Around 1,832,482
Roman Baths	Bath	845,608
Stonehenge	Amesbury	759,697
Dart Pleasure Craft Limited	Dartmouth	721,822
Bristol Zoo Gardens	Clifton	574,122
Longleat Estate	Warminster	492,807
Woodlands Leisure Park	Blackawton	Around 400,000
National Marine Aquarium	Plymouth	Around 380,000

THE UK'S TOP TEN HOUSE PLANTS BY POPULARITY

1. Spring bulbs
2. Peace lily (*Spathiphyllum*)
3. Orchid
4. Ferns
5. African violet (*Saintpaulia*)
6. Azalea
7. Palm
8. Cyclamen
9. Poinsettia
10. Cacti and succulents

ANARCHY IN NOTTINGHAM

Nottingham Magistrates Court enjoyed its finest moment when The Sex Pistols appeared there in 1977, accused (under the 1899 Indecent Advertisements Act) for the supposedly obscene use of the word 'bollocks' in the title of their album *Never Mind The Bollocks Here's The Sex Pistols*. They were defended by John 'Rumpole of the Bailey' Mortimer QC and won the case.

CANAL SURPRISE

There are more kilometres of canal in Birmingham than there are in Venice.

THE UNKNOWN ALTON TOWERS

Alton Towers is one of the UK's most popular theme parks, but the site, set in 202 hectares (500 acres) of superbly landscaped grounds in the heart of Staffordshire, dates back as far as the eighth century, when the Towers site became a fortress held by Ceolred, King of Mercia. The earls of Shrewsbury occupied the castle from 1412, when Lady Ankarat de Verdun married Sir John Talbot. The Shrewsbury title remained in the same family until the 1920s.

A ROYAL WAGER

To finance his tobacco cultivation trip to America, Sir Walter Raleigh bet Queen Elizabeth I that he could calculate the weight of smoke. He did this by placing two identical cigars on opposite sides of a scale, then he lit one of the cigars, making sure no ashes fell. The difference in the weight after the cigar was done was therefore the weight of smoke…and Raleigh was on his way to America.

PLAGUE TOWN

The Great Plague swept through Britain like wildfire in 1665. In the village of Eyam, in Derbyshire, the epidemic (in which five out of every six villagers died) is said to have arrived in a plague-infested box of laundry. The courage of the doomed villagers and of their rector, William Mompesson – who survived – is no legend. Once the disease began to claim its victims, Mompesson persuaded his parishioners to isolate themselves from the outside world and therefore prevent the plague from spreading to other communities.

UP, UP AND AWAY

Northampton racecourse is home to the famous annual balloon festival, which features more than 90 balloons. The three-day festival has been established for 11 years and now attracts around 250,000 visitors. The event features fireworks, attractions and the amazing evening 'balloon glow'.

SCURVY KNAVES!

English sailors became known as Limeys after using lime juice to combat scurvy – a disease that is caused by a lack of vitamin C, which is abundant in citrus fruit.

MILLION UP

London was the first city in the world to have a population of more than 1 million.

SOME FACTS ABOUT THE CLIFTON SUSPENSION BRIDGE

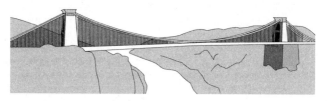

Total span between the towers: 214m (702ft)

Height above high water level: 75m (245ft)

Since its opening in 1864, meticulous maintenance has ensured that the bridge has never closed. The structure – designed in the 1830s, built in the 1860s and intended entirely for horse-drawn traffic – now carries a staggering total of 4 million cars a year.

There have been over 1,000 suicides since the bridge opened.

In 1885, after a lovers' tiff, Sarah Ann Henley jumped off the bridge. Her billowing skirts acted as a parachute, checking her fall, and she landed in the river. Although she was severely injured, Sarah recovered and died in her eighties.

The first aeroplane to fly under the bridge was that of Frenchman M Tetard in 1911. In spite of a later ban on such escapades, in 1957 a pilot of 501 Squadron, at nearby Filton, took his Vampire jet beneath the bridge at a speed of 720kph (450mph), only to crash into the side of the gorge. He was killed instantly.

The road level of Clifton Suspension Bridge is almost 1m (3ft) higher at the Clifton end than at the Leigh Woods end. Brunel incorporated this into the design, to give the bridge the appearance of being absolutely horizontal when seen from a distance.

BRITAIN'S SMALLEST COUNTY

Rutland was Britain's smallest county until it was swallowed up by Leicestershire in the 1974 local government shake-up. But it lives on thanks to Rutland Water, which was created by damming the Gwash River in 1970, and by former Monty Python Eric Idle's TV spoof, *Rutland Weekend TV* (which also spawned his Beatles parody, *The Rutles*.)

WATER SPORTS

Nottinghamshire is home to the National Water Sports Centre, at Holme Pierrepont. It is Britain's first purpose-built multi-water-sports centre, with facilities specially designed to meet the national requirements of rowing, canoeing and waterskiing.

EMAIL MA'AM

The words 'electronic mail' might sound new, but in fact the email was introduced 30 years ago. Queen Elizabeth II sent her first email in 1976.

LEFT-HAND DRIVE

About a quarter of the world drives on the left-hand side of the road, and the countries that still do so are mostly old British colonies.

GEORGE ORWELL'S GUIDE TO THE PERFECT CUPPA

1. Use tea from India or Ceylon (Sri Lanka), not China.

2. Use a teapot, preferably ceramic.

3. Warm the pot over direct heat.

4. Tea should be strong – six spoons of leaves per 1 litre (2 pints).

5. Let the leaves move around the pot – no bags or strainers.

6. Take the pot to the boiling kettle.

7. Stir or shake the pot.

8. Drink out of a tall, mug-shaped teacup.

9. Don't add creamy milk.

10. Add milk to the tea, not vice versa.

11. Do not add sugar.

HELLO?

Alexander Graham Bell, inventor of the telephone, never phoned his wife or mother to tell them of his success, because they were both deaf.

SILBURY HILL

Silbury Hill, constructed in 2700 BC, is the largest artificial mound in Europe. It stands 40m (130ft) high, while its base covers an area of 2.2 hectares (5.4 acres). Thought to be the burial place of a great tribal leader, its sheer size has defied every excavation attempt.

JIMI'S LAST STAND

Now private apartments, the Samarkand Hotel, at 22 Lansdowne Crescent, Holland Park, achieved notoriety in 1970 when one of its guests, guitarist Jimi Hendrix, was found dead after an overdose of sleeping pills.

SEX EDUCATION

The average age for first sex is now 16, though 30 per cent of boys and 26 per cent of girls do not hang around that long. More than 90,000 teenagers get pregnant every year. (In 2002, 7,700 were under 16 and 2,200 under 14.)

LIFE EXPECTANCY IN THE UK

Total population: 78.16 years
Males: 75.74 years
Females: 80.70 years

HIS MASTER'S VOICE OPENS FOR BUSINESS

Now claiming to be the largest music retailer in the world, HMV opened its first shop at 363 Oxford Street, London, in July 1921. The ribbon was cut by well-known old groover Edward Elgar.

DEAD CHEAP

To save costs, the body of Shakespeare's friend and fellow dramatist, Ben Jonson, was buried (in 1637) standing up in Westminster Abbey.

LONDON: A MUSICAL TOP 40

Here is a list of 40 songs that made the UK Top 40.

'London Town', The Pretty Things (1965)
'London Boys', David Bowie (1966)
'London Conversation', John Martyn (1968)
'London Blues', Canned Heat (1970)
'London Berry Blues', Chuck Berry (1972)
'A Souvenir Of London', Procul Harum (1973)
'Streets Of London', Ralph McTell (1974)
'London Luck And Love', Hall and Oates (1976)
'London Boy', T-Rex (1976)
'London's Burning', The Clash (1977)
'London Traffic', The Jam (1977)
'London Girl', The Jam (1977)
'Red London', Sham 69 (1977)
'London Lady', Stranglers (1977)
'London Girls', Vibrators (1977)
'London Town', Wings (1978)
'Werewolves Of London', Warren Zevon (1978)
'London Calling', The Clash (1979)
'Last Train To London', ELO (1979)
'Barmy London Army', Charlie Harper (1980)
'London Town', Light Of The World (1980)
'Towers Of London', XTC (1980)
'Dark Streets Of London', The Pogues (1984)
'Tower Of London', ABC (1985)
'London Girl', The Pogues (1986)
'London', The Smiths (1987)
'Lullaby Of London', The Pogues (1988)
'London Bridge', Big Audio Dynamite (1989)
'Down To London', Joe Jackson (1989)
'London Kid', Jean-Michel Jarre (1989)
'London You're A Lady', The Pogues (1989)
'London Belongs To Me', St Etienne (1991)
'Everything's Changed Since You Been To London', Kingmaker (1992)
'P 25 London', Black Crowes (1994)
'London Loves', Blur (1994)
'London's Brilliant Parade', Elvis Costello (1994)
'London Can You Wait?', Gene (1994)
'Londinium', Archive (1996)
'London Tonight', Collapsed Lung (1996)
'In And Out In Paris And London', Divine Comedy (1996)

EALING'S GLORY YEARS

Ealing Studios are best known for their run of now-classic comedies from the late 1940s and early 1950s, though their very 'Englishness', their quirks and idiosyncrasies, often led to them being dismissed as twee and stereotyped. This is missing the point, however, for the company originated in the early sound era, and from 1938 – under the stewardship of Michael Balcon (Daniel Day Lewis' grandfather) – produced many fine films that deserve to be better known.

The studios were (and still are) located at Ealing Green, in west London. In 1929, London theatre producer Basil Dean formed Associated Radio Pictures and raised finance to build the Ealing Studios, which were completed two years later. The site was only metres away from the early Will Barker Studios, which had opened in 1896. The studios were the first purpose-built sound stage in Britain, and altogether about 60 pictures were made there between 1931 and 1938. The National Film and Television School purchased Ealing Studios in 1995.

EH? PLACE NAMES THAT DO NOT LOOK HOW THEY SOUND

Name	Pronounced
Balquhidder	Balhwidder
Beauchamp	Beacham
Belvoir	Beaver
Bicester	Bister
Cirencester	Sissister (until about 1850)
Conduit	Kundit
Fowey	Foy
Hunstanton	Hunston
Kircudbright	Kircoobree
Leicester	Lester
Leominster	Lemster
Lympne	Limm
Mousehole	Mouzel
St John	Sinjun
Ulgham	Uffham
Wymondham	Windum
Zwill	Yool

TEN CRACKING CAVES (AND WHY)

Bruce's Cave, Kirkpatrick Fleming, Dumfries and Galloway (where Robert the Bruce allegedly watched the spider)

Cathedral Cav, Pen-Y-Cae, Breconshire (magnificent illuminations)

Cheddar Gorge, Somerset (Cox's cave)

Redcliffe Caves, Bristol (a maze of underground tunnels)

Royston Cave, Royston, Hertfordshire (ancient wall sculptures)

St Clement's Cave, Hastings, Sussex (once the haunt of illicit gamblers)

Speedwell Cavern, Castleton, Derbyshire (underground boat trip)

West Wycombe Caves, West Wycombe, Buckinghamshire (spooky waxworks and the 'Inner Temple')

White Scar Caves, Ingleton, Yorkshire (underground river and waterfalls)

Wookey Hole Caves, Somerset (Goatsherd Chamber, Witches' Parlour, and Witch's Kitchen)

THE SOUTHWEST'S TOP VISITOR ATTRACTIONS (FREE)

Attraction	Location	Visitors
Truro Cathedral	Truro	Around 500,000
Arnolfini Gallery	Bristol	482,275
Cornish Cyder Farm	Penhallow	355,000
Bristol City Museum and Art Gallery	Bristol	311,890
Wells Cathedral	Wells	Around 300,000
Cheddar Gorge Cheese Company	Cheddar Gorge	Around 300,000
Donkey Sanctuary	Salcombe Regis	Around 250,000
Trago Mills	Liverton	Around 240,000
Teign Valley Glass and House of Marbles	Bovey Tracey	Around 200,000

THE BIG HAND SAYS: WHEN IT'S 12:00 GMT IN THE UK, IT'S...

1:00pm
Algiers, Amsterdam, Belgrade, Berlin, Berne, Brussels, Budapest, Copenhagen, Lagos, Madrid, Oslo, Paris, Rome, Warsaw

2:00pm
Athens, Beirut, Bucharest, Cairo, Cape Town, Helsinki, Jerusalem

3:00pm
Istanbul, Moscow

5:00pm
Karachi, Madras

5:30pm
Bombay, Calcutta

7:00pm
Lima

8:00pm
Beijing, Hong Kong, Singapore

9:00pm
Tokyo

10:00pm
Sydney

Midnight
Auckland

2:00am
Melbourne

4:00am
San Francisco

6:00am
Chicago

7:00am
New York

Midday
Lisbon

FACTS ABOUT STONEHENGE

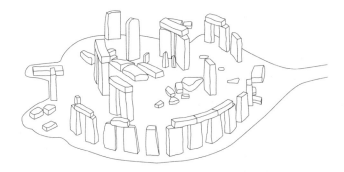

The triptychs at Stonehenge, in Wiltshire, are one of the great wonders of the ancient world. However, the surrounding area has always been of great significance for early man. Within 16km (10 miles) of the site there are 12 long barrows constructed from 4000 BC onwards and more than 200 round barrows dating from 2000 BC onwards.

Uniquely, the stones at Stonehenge were pounded and shaped to fit the structures the builders wanted to create. The earliest structure was a ditch with a circle of 56 pits known as Aubrey Holes, which was built between 2800 BC and 2300 BC. Around 80 huge sarcen stones, some weighing up to 51 tonnes (56 tons), were hauled to the site from Marlborough Down. Much of the construction was carried out by a tribe known as the Beaker Folk.

1–10 OF NUMERICAL UK PLACE NAMES

Once Brewed, Northumberland
Two Bridges, Devon
Three Cocks, Powys
Four Ashes, Warwickshire
Five Penny Borve, Isle of Lewis
Sixpenny Handley, Dorset
Seven Bridges, Wiltshire
Eight Ash Green, Suffolk
Nine Mile Burn, Lothian
Ten Mile Bank, Cambridgeshire

WHERE ON EARTH? SOME UNUSUAL UK PLACE NAMES

Ugley, Suffolk
Great Snoring, Norfolk
Yelling, Cambridgeshire
Maggieknockater, Grampian
Wyre Piddle, Worcestershire
Wrangle, Lincolnshire
Nutt's Corner, Belfast
Stewponey, West Midlands
Six Mile Bottom, Cambridgeshire

INTERNET PORN

More than a third of UK Web surfers are taking a peek at X-rated websites, according to a BBC survey

JUST DON'T ASK FOR PORK SCRATCHINGS

Once the haunt of notorious highwaymen, The Hatchet Inn, established in 1606, is Bristol's oldest public house. The 300-year-old main door is said to have layers of human skin under the tar, and many large offers have been made for it (but all have been declined). Cock fighting and boxing have both been staged there, and bare-knuckle fights involving 'All-England Champions' attracted enormous purses in days gone by.

ROCHESTER'S CITY LIMITS

The Kent town of Rochester gained city status in 1211, but a bizarre administrative error in 1998 – in which a council official failed to fill in a government form correctly – meant that Rochester lost its city status!

MORSE CODE

Thanks to global sales, it is estimated that around a billion people around the world have watched an episode of *Inspector Morse.*

IRISH INVASION?

In 1870, there were more Irish living in London than in Dublin. There were also more Catholics living in London than in Rome.

THE ROMANS IN BRITAIN: THEIR NAMES FOR OUR TOWNS

Aldeburgh	Isurium
Bath	Aquae Sulis
Brough	Peturaria
Caerleon	Isca silurum
Caerwent	Vents silurum
Canterbury	Durovernum
Carlisle	Luguvalium
Chelmsford	Caesaromagus
Chester	Deva
Chichester	Noviomagus
Cirencester	Corinium
Colchester	Camulodunum
Doncaster	Danum
Dorchester	Durnovaria
Dover	Dubris
Exeter	Isca Dumnoniorum
Gloucester	Glevum
Lancaster	Lunecastrum
Leicester	Ratae Coritanorum
Lincoln	Lindum
London	Londinium
Manchester	Mancunium
Newcastle	Pons Aelius
Newstead	Trimontium
Pevensey	Anderida
Rochester	Durobrivae
St Albans	Verulamium
Salisbury	Sorbiodunum
Silchester	Calleva Atrebatum
Winchester	Venta Belgarum
Worcester	Wigornia
Wroxeter	Viroconium
Yarmouth	Magna Gernemutha
York	Eboracum

BRITAIN – THAT'S ABOUT THE SIZE OF IT

England 130,440 square km (50,363 square miles); **Scotland** 78,760 square km (30,409 square miles); **Wales** 20,770 square km (8,019 square miles); **Northern Ireland** 14,123 square km (5,453 square miles).

ALL RISE: THE NATIONAL ANTHEM

It's believed that the National Anthem became linked to royal events in 1745, when it was played to mark George II's defeat by the Scots at Prestonpans. Thankfully, only the first verse is now sung to mark royal occasions.

God save our gracious Queen,
Long live our noble Queen,
God save the Queen!
Send her victorious, happy and glorious,
Long to reign over us;
God save the Queen!

O Lord our God arise,
Scatter her enemies
And make them fall;
Confound their politics, frustrate their knavish tricks,
On thee our hopes we fix,
God save us all!

Thy choicest gifts in store,
On her be pleased to pour,
Long may she reign;
May she defend our laws, and give us ever cause
To sing with heart and voice,
God save the Queen!

Not in this land alone,
But be God's mercies known
From shore to shore!
Lord make the nations see, that we should brothers be
And form one family,
The wide world over.

From every latent foe,
From the assassin's blow,
God save the Queen!
O'er her thine arm extend, for Britain's sake defend
Our mother, prince and friend,
God save the Queen!

HOW TO GET FROM LAND'S END TO JOHN O'GROATS IN 1,336KM (835 MILES) AND 16 HOURS (APPROXIMATELY)

Join the A30 at Trevescan – join the M5 at junction 31 south of Exeter – join the M6 at West Bromwich towards Stoke on Trent – exit Junction 44 Carlisle north, join the A74 – join A74(M) at junction 22 near Gretna – A74(M) becomes M74 at junction 13 at Abington – at junction 4, join M73 north – at junction 3, join A80 east – at junction 4, join M80 north – join M9 towards Perth – at junction 11, join the A9 and continue north – turn on to the A99 at Latherton – continue past Wick, Keiss and the stacks of Duncansby – arrive John O'Groats

BRITAIN'S OLDEST UNIVERSITY

The University of Oxford was the first to be established in Britain. Dating from the 12th century, it is organised as a federation of colleges that are governed by their own teaching staff, known as 'fellows'. The oldest college, University College, was founded in 1249. Other notable colleges include All Souls (founded in 1438), Christ Church (founded in 1546 by Cardinal Wolsey), and Lady Margaret Hall (founded in 1878), the first women's college. Today, Oxford University is made up of 35 separate colleges, of which two are for women students only (the rest enrol both men and women).

BOUDICCA'S REVENGE

In AD 60, Queen Boudicca and her Iceni tribe swept down against the Roman garrison of Colchester, which was at the time the Romans' main colony in Britain. It was weakly defended – partly because the British had previously ambushed and killed 1,500 Romans marching to reinforce the town. Its tiny garrison held out for two days, but when it fell there was wholesale destruction and slaughter. The layer of ash left by the massive fires can still be found on archaeological digs.

HOLIDAY FACT

The most popular pastime for overseas holidaymakers in Britain is visiting heritage sites.

THE AMAZING CHANNEL TUNNEL

Early plans for a link between the UK and the European continent included chains of bridges linked to artificial islands built in the Channel and submerged tubes chained to the seabed.

The first recognisable tunnel plan was put forward by Frenchman Albert Mathieu-Favier in 1802.

Excavation work was attempted on several occasions in the next 200 years, but were invariably shelved because of the expense.

On 12 February 1986, an agreement was signed between the French and British governments that allowed private investors to create companies and run the Channel Tunnel between Folkestone and Calais.

Work began on 1 July 1987 and the first of three linkages was completed on 30 October 1990.

The Channel Tunnel is the second longest in the world.

The distance between the two entrances is 49.94km (31.03 miles) – of that, 37km (23 miles) is underwater.

The maximum depth reached below the seabed is 70m (230ft).

Excavating the three tunnels generated 7 million cubic m (246 million cubic ft) of spoil.

THE MEANING OF BLIGHTY

'Blighty' is another nickname for Britain. In World War I, soldiers would pray for a 'blighty' – a wound that would get them back to 'Blighty' for treatment. Some people say that it's a corruption of 'beauty', but more probably it's derived from a Hindu word meaning 'stranger' that was picked up when India was under British rule.

BLIMPS

It used to be said that there were more retired colonels in Hythe per square kilometre than there were anywhere else in the country.

BODLEY'S GIFT

Oxford University's Bodleian Library – founded in 1602, with a bequest of 2,000 books by Sir Thomas Bodley – is the oldest library in Britain and now contains more than 4 million books.

THE STORY OF ST ALBAN

Britain's first Christian martyr was a Roman soldier called Alban, who was in fact crucified by his Roman comrades for harbouring a Christian in the town of Verulamium in AD 209. The spot where he died is now the site of the Abbey of St Alban, and 900 years after his death Verulamium was renamed St Albans.

THE DUNMOW FLITCH

First recorded in 1244, the Dunmow Flitch is a bizarre competition, held every Whit Monday in the Essex town of Dunmow (a flitch is a whole side of pork). Married couples can nominate themselves for the award, providing they can convince a jury of the truth of the following statement: 'Having been married for at least a year and a day, we have never once, sleeping or waking, regretted our marriage or wished ourselves single again.'

BRITAIN'S HIGH AND LOW POINTS

Lowest point is in the Fens: −4m (−13ft)

Highest point is Ben Nevis: 1,343m (4,406ft)

BLACKBURN, LANCASHIRE: ITS HOLES

A story in the *Lancashire Evening Telegraph* about council officials counting the exact number of potholes in Blackburn (there were 4,000) inspired John Lennon to write the opening lines of 'Day In The Life', featured on the *Sergeant Pepper* album.

EXPLAINED: THOSE BAFFLING ENGLISH PHRASES

'The whole nine yards'
This originated in the World War I. A Lewis machine gun boasted a nine-yard magazine belt, so 'to give them the whole nine yards' suggested using up an entire belt on the enemy.

'Don't throw the baby out with the bath water'
In medieval times, people usually took one bath a year. The man of the house had the privilege of nice, clean hot water. Then it was the turn of all the other men of the household; then the women; and then the children. Last of all were the babies (but by then the water was so dirty you could actually lose someone in it).

EXPLAINED: THOSE BAFFLING ENGLISH PHRASES (CONT'D)

'Bloody'
This very common swearing word is a shortened form of 'By God's blood'.

'It's raining cats and dogs'
Old houses had thatched roofs, which also happened to be the only place for household pets to get warm. When it rained, it became slippery, and sometimes the animals would slip and fall off the roof.

'Mind your p's and q's'
Ale was (and still is) drunk in pints and quarts. So, when customers got unruly, the innkeeper would yell at them to mind their own pints and quarts, and settle down.

'Wet your whistle'
Many years ago, frequenters of pubs had a whistle baked into the rim or handle of their ceramic mugs, so when they needed a refill they used the whistle to get some service. 'Wet your whistle' is the phrase inspired by this practice.

'Goodnight, sleep tight'
In Shakespeare's time, mattresses were secured on bed frames by ropes. When you pulled on the ropes the mattress tightened, which made the bed firmer to sleep on.

'One for the road'
During the Middle Ages and medieval period, the condemned were taken from London city jails to Tyburn Hill for execution. En route, along what is today's Oxford Street, the cart stopped and they were allowed one final drink at a country inn situated on the road. The 'one' they were drinking was for the road to death.

'Show a leg'
Apparently, when the ships of old were about to leave port, the sailors might have tried to smuggle a lady aboard, concealing her in their hammock. The officers or mates would do a final inspection of the ship and crew before she left, and anybody in a hammock was bidden to 'show a leg'. Should a hairless and shapely one dangle, the owner was usually a Jill (not Jack) Tar, and eviction swiftly followed!

THE LAST BATTLE

The last battle to take place on English soil occurred at Sedgemoor on 6 July 1685, when James, Duke of Monmouth, was defeated by Royalist forces.

THE HISTORY OF BLACKPOOL

1735 The first recorded visitors to Blackpool stay at Ethart A Whiteside's cottage. In those days, Blackpool was an insignificant little fishing village.

1750 The first amusement arcade, Uncle Tom's Cabin, opens up.

1846 The first railway is completed.

1863 The first pier (North Pier) opens.

1885 The first electric tramway is opened.

1894 Blackpool Tower is opened.

1994 Blackpool attracts 16.8 million visitors a year, generating £435 million ($720 million) – more than all the Greek islands and mainland Greece combined. There are 3,500 hotels, guesthouses and holiday flats containing 120,000 holiday beds (more than the whole of Portugal).

A BRIDGE TOO FAR?

From west to east London, The Thames is spanned by the following bridges: Kew, Chiswick, Barnes, Hammersmith, Putney, Wandsworth, Battersea, Albert, Chelsea, Vauxhall, Lambeth, Westminster, Hungerford Foot Bridge, Waterloo, Blackfriars, Millennium Foot Bridge, Southwark, London, Tower (Rotherhithe Tunnel, Greenwich Foot Tunnel, Blackwall Tunnel).

WHAT A WAY TO GO!

King Edward II was deposed in the 14th century, to be succeeded by his son, Edward III. The king was imprisoned in Berkeley Castle and there were instructions that no one should harm him and, when the decision was made to murder him, that no mark should be left on the body. A deer horn was therefore inserted into his rectum and a red-hot poker placed inside that. They say that his ghostly screams can still be heard in the castle.

THE MIRACLE OF SKARA BRAE

In the winter of 1850, a great storm battered Orkney. There's nothing particularly unusual about that, but on this occasion the combination of Orkney's notorious winds and extremely high tides stripped the grass from a large mound known as Skara Brae. This revealed the outline of a series of stone buildings that intrigued the local laird, William Watt of Skaill, who began an excavation of the site.

By 1868, the remains of four ancient houses had been unearthed but Skara Brae was abandoned, and remained undisturbed until 1925, when another storm damaged some of the previously excavated structures. At the time, the village was thought to be an Iron Age settlement, but radiocarbon dating in the early 1970s showed that it actually dated from the late Neolithic period, inhabited between 3200 and 2200 BC.

Because of the protection offered by the sand cocooning the settlement for 4,000 years, these buildings and their contents are incredibly well-preserved. The walls of the huts are still standing, and alleyways still have roofs with their original stone slabs.

COSMOPOLITAN BRITAIN?

Despite the influx of immigrants into Britain since the end of World War II, the following table shows that English is still very much the predominant nationality in the UK:

English	81.5 per cent
Scottish	9.6 per cent
Irish	2.4 per cent
Welsh	1.9 per cent
Northern Irish	1.8 per cent
West Indian, Indian, Pakistani and other	2.8 per cent.

RELIGIONS IN BRITAIN

1	Anglican/Roman Catholic	40 million
2	Muslim	1.5 million
3	Presbyterian	800,000
4	Methodist	760,000
5	Sikh	500,000
6	Hindu	500,000
7	Jewish	350,000

SAY CHEESE

There are over 400 British cheeses. These are the most popular:

1 Caerphilly
2 Wensleydale
3 Lancashire
4 Mild Cheddar
5 Medium Cheddar
6 Mature Cheddar
7 Vintage Cheddar
8 Double Gloucester
9 Red Leicester
10 Stilton
11 White Cheshire
12 Coloured Cheshire
13 Derby
14 Sage Derby
15 Shropshire Blue
16 White Stilton, White Stilton with apricots, and White Stilton with cranberries
17 Dovedale
18 Buxton Blue
19 British Brie
20 Cornish Yarg

LAND OF EDEN

The Eden Project is located in a former clay pit near St Austell, Cornwall. It consists of three huge 'biomes', housing conservatories with plants from around the world. Boardwalks lead visitors through 12,000 plants, taking them from the Oceanic Islands to Malaysia and from West Africa to South America. Erecting the covered biomes took the largest birdcage scaffolding in the world. It extends over 12 levels, measures 25m (82ft) across, and involved 46,000 poles of scaffolding, totalling 370km (230 miles).

The scaffolding has entered *The Guinness Book Of World Records*. The largest biome is 240m (790ft) long, 55m (180ft) high and 110m (360ft) wide, and has no internal supports. It is large enough to house the Tower of London, could fit a tower 11 double-decker buses high, and is the length of a nose-to-nose traffic jam of 24 buses.

SOUTHWEST RECORD BREAKERS

Longest sea bar: Chesil Beach, Dorset – 15km (10 miles)
Largest gorge: Cheddar Gorge, Somerset – 150m (500ft)
Oldest theatre: Theatre Royal, Bristol – 1766
Tallest lighthouse: Bishop's Rock, Isle of Scilly – 47.8m (156.8ft)
Largest maze: Longleat House, Warminster – 0.6 hectares (1.48 acres)

THREE THINGS YOU NEVER KNEW ABOUT EXETER

The present Exeter Cathedral dates from 1275 and features the longest stretch of Gothic vaulting in Britain – more than 90m (300ft).

The city's Guildhall was built in 1468. It continues to be inhabited by Exeter City Council, and is the oldest municipal building in England still in use.

Exeter's ship canal, built in 1566, is the oldest in Britain – thanks to Isabella de Fortibus (Countess of Devon), who, following a land dispute several years earlier, had built a weir across the busy River Exe to cut off the city's trading route to the sea.

WATCH YOUR STEP IN MAYFAIR

A good deal of the land is London is still owned by the Crown and a handful of rich families. The largest and most lucrative of these historic estates is that of the Grosvenors, much of whose land is in Mayfair and Belgravia. Part of the reason that this area looks so smart is because the Grosvenor estate exercises strict control over the upkeep of properties, ensuring they are all regularly painted in a magnolia cream colour, don't have satellite dishes and (in some cases) display their coat of arms.

RINGS FOR ALL SEASONS

The famous Maumbury Rings are to be found near Dorchester. These were originally built in the Stone Age as a ritual stone circle, but have come in handy since then. The Romans converted the circle into a 10,000-seat amphitheatre for gladiatorial contests, and in medieval times the amphitheatre became the site of jousting, bear baiting and cock fighting. In the 17th and 18th centuries, the crowds flocked there to see public executions.

RUDE MAN OF CERNE

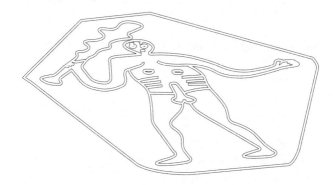

Standing at 55m (180ft) tall, with a 37m (120ft) knobbly club and a whopping 10m (33ft) penis, the Cerne Abbas giant – otherwise known as the Rude Man of Cerne – is an unmistakable tourist attraction north of Dorchester. During prudish Victorian times, the trenches of the giant's penis were filled with dirt and hidden beneath grass. The giant, whose name may derive from the Celtic fertility god Cernunnos, has the legendary power to cure barrenness in women, and childless couples still copulate while lying on the grass in the giant's phallus. A sight line taken up the giant's penis on May Day points directly at the sun as it rises over the crest of the hill.

SOME FASCINATING FACTS ABOUT ALTON TOWERS RIDES

The AIR ride reportedly cost £12 million ($20 million) to create and reaches a maximum speed of 73kph (46mph)!

A car on Nemesis travels 30,000km (19,000 miles) a season – that's enough to take it three-quarters of the way round the world!

On average, an Oblivion shuttle drops 14km (8 3/4 miles) a day – enough to go to Monaco and back in a season!

If you brave Nemesis, you will experience a greater G-force than a NASA astronaut – Nemesis reaches 4G, while NASA reaches a paltry 3G!

WORD UP

The average person's vocabulary is between 10,000 and 15,000 words. Shakespeare had more than 29,000 words up his sleeve, however.

FASCINATING FACTS ABOUT THE *OXFORD ENGLISH DICTIONARY*

Number of headwords: 300,000

Number of words and phrases covered: 640,000

Number of quotations: 2.5 million

Number of words of text: 60 million

Most-quoted male author: William Shakespeare

Most-quoted female author: George Eliot

Most-quoted work: the Bible

Most-quoted 20-century author: James Joyce

Longest word: 'pneumonoultramicroscopicsilicovolcanoconiosis', a factitious word alleged to mean 'a lung disease caused by the inhalation of very fine silica dust' (but occurs chiefly as an instance of a very long word!)

Longest entry: the verb 'set' (60,000 words)

Shortest entry: 'm. Var. MA'AM'

Letter containing the largest number of headwords: S

Letter containing the smallest number of headwords: X

ANIMALS AT THE TOWER

The Tower of London was once used as a zoo, and housed a menagerie of all kinds of animals, including lions. The moat used to have water in it, but was drained in 1843. During World War II, it was used to grow vegetables.

A WELL-FORTIFIED CASTLE

Dartmouth Castle, built in 1495, was the first in Britain designed specifically for artillery, with gun ports rather than arrow slits built into the walls.

BATH FACTS

The Roman spa baths are a major tourist attraction in Bath. The springs produce 1 million litres (265,000 gallons) of water every day at a constant temperature of 48°C (118°F).

FILTHY ENGLISH!

In a 2003 survey, a third of British people said they picked their nose more than five times a day, and many admitted that they did not change their underwear daily.

Researchers found that 34 per cent of respondents had no shame in burping loudly in public and that 29 per cent would pass wind indiscreetly.

Only 3 per cent of the men in Kent who were questioned admitted changing their underwear every day, compared to 78 per cent of Welsh men and 55 per cent of women in Dorset.

Northern Ireland has the most number of bad habits in the UK: 44 per cent confess to picking their nose more than five times a day. The region also topped the league for belching the most in public (44 per cent) and passing wind (34 per cent).

Half of the male respondents from Essex said they deliberately burped or passed wind loudly in public.

Women from Dorset were not portrayed very well by the survey: half admitted picking their nose and a similar number confessed to belching and passing wind loudly in public.

THE BIRTH OF THE POTTERIES

An abundance of water, marl, clay and easily mined coal (to fire the kilns) enabled Staffordshire to develop as a ceramics centre. In the 18th century, pottery became widely accessible and affordable, and in 1910 the six towns of Longton, Fenton, Hanley, Burslam, Tunstall and Stoke-on-Trent merged to form the conurbation also known as the Potteries.

BAR BAIRD

Inventor John Logie Baird first demonstrated how television would work above what is now Bar Italia on Frith Street, in the middle of Soho, London.

THE MIDLANDS' TOP VISITOR ATTRACTIONS (PAID)

Attraction	Location	Visitors in 2002
Drayton Manor Family Theme Park	Tamworth	Around 1,200,000
Chatsworth	Bakewell	620,210
Cadbury World	Bournville	534,766
Twycross Zoo	Twycross	436,907
Shakespeare's Birthplace	Stratford-upon-Avon	373,654
Waterworld	Etruria	352,000

SOME ILLUMINATING FACTS ABOUT BLACKPOOL LIGHTS

Although Blackpool's famous illuminations first appeared in 1933, it was not until 1934 that a proper switching-on ceremony was devised to launch the summer season's grand finale. Lord Derby did the honours, followed by this impressive roll call of celebrities:

1935 Audrey Mossom (Railway Queen)
1936 Sir Josiah Stamp
1937 Alderman Ashton (later Duke of Kent)
1938 Councillor Mrs Quayle
1939 Cancelled when war broke out – no display during war years or, indeed, until...
1949 Anna Neagle
1950 Wilfred Pickles
1951 Stanley Mathews
1952 Valerie Hobson
1953 George Formby
1954 Gilbert Harding
1955 Jacob Malik (Russian Ambassador)
1956 Reginald Dixon
1957 John H Whitney (American Ambassador)
1958 AE 'Matt' Matthews
1959 Jane Mansfield
1960 Janet Munro
1961 Violet Carson
1962 Shirley Anne Field
1963 Cliff Michelmore

1964 Gracie Fields
1965 David Tomlinson
1966 Ken Dodd
1967 Dr Horace King (Speaker)
1968 Sir Matt Busby
1969 Canberra Bomber
1970 Tony Blackburn
1971 Cast of *Dad's Army*
1972 Danny La Rue
1973 Gordon Banks
1974 Wendy Craig
1975 Tom Baker (*Dr Who*)
1976 Carol Ann Grant (Miss United Kingdom)
1977 Red Rum (Grand National winner – a horse!)
1978 Terry Wogan
1979 Kermit the Frog and the Muppets
1980 Cannon and Ball
1981 Earl and Countess Spencer
1982 Rear Admiral 'Sandy' Woodward
1983 Doris Speed and cast of *Coronation Street*
1984 Johannes Rau (Minister-President, North Rhine Westphalia) and
      David Waddington, QC, MP (Minister of State, Home Office)
1985 Joanna Lumley, BBC *Children In Need*
1986 Les Dawson
1987 Frank Bough, Ann Gregg and Kathy Tayler (BBC *Holiday* programme)
1988 Andrew Lloyd Webber and Sarah Brightman
1989 Frank Bruno
1990 Julie Goodyear and Roy Barraclough (Bet and Alec Gilroy,
      Coronation Street)
1991 Derek Jameson and Judith Chalmers
1992 Lisa Stansfield
1993 Status Quo and Radio One
1994 Shirley Bassey
1995 Bee Gees and Radio One
1996 Eternal and Radio One
1997 Michael Ball and Radio Two
1998 Chris De Burgh and Radio Two
1999 Gary Barlow and Radio Two
2000 Westlife and Radio Two
2001 Steps and Radio Two
2002 Ronan Keating and Radio Two
2003 Blue and Radio Two

ELEANOR RIGBY'S STATUE

The statue of Eleanor Rigby is situated on a bench in Stanley Street, Liverpool, in honour of the eponymous heroine of The Beatles' song. It was sculpted by Tommy Steele, the UK's first rock 'n' roll star of the 1950s, who donated the statue, which was unveiled in December 1982, for 'half a sixpence' (the title of one of his hits). Inside the statue he placed a four-leaf clover, a pair of football boots, a page from the Bible, an adventure book and a Shakespeare sonnet. Crazy, man!

TOTP

The former Wesleyan chapel on Dickenson Road, Rusholme, gained legendary status when it became the site of the first ever broadcast of *Top Of The Pops* on New Year's Day 1964. Hosted by Jimmy Savile, the bill included The Rolling Stones, Dusty Springfield, The Hollies, The Dave Clark Five and The Swinging Blue Jeans. The show was only supposed to run for six weeks, but, 40 years later, it is probably safe to say the idea caught on! The chapel was not so lucky: when the show moved to London in 1967, it was demolished and replaced by a telephone exchange.

STRANGEWAYS

Manchester's imposing prison, built in the Victorian era, is famous for being the place where, in August 1964, John Walby (aka Gwynne Evans) became the last person to be hanged in Britain.

FIRST CANAL IN BRITAIN

There are several claimants to this title, including the Roman Fossdyke at Lincoln (AD 100), the Sankey Brook Navigation and the Exeter Navigation Canal (both 1600s), but the first 'artificial watercourse for inland navigation' was built in 1761. The Duke of Bridgewater's Canal, constructed by James Brindley, was designed to transport coal from the duke's coalmines at Worsley across country to Manchester. The canal even crosses the River Irwell by viaduct.

CHINESE WHISPERS

The Imperial Arch, centrepiece of Manchester's Chinatown district, is the largest Chinese gateway in Europe. It stands 9.2m (30ft) tall and was built by a team specially flown in from Beijing.

SCOUSE

Scouse – or, to give it its full title, Lobscouse – is a food rather than a dialect, the native dish of the Liverpudlian (or Scouser). It is to Liverpool what bouillabaisse is to Marseilles or schnitzel is to Vienna. Unlike most dishes, which derive from a place of origin, Scouse was born out of abject poverty, and is a simple stew made from the cheapest cuts of meat (usually mutton), boiled with potatoes and onions. The meat ingredient is optional, without which a Scouse becomes Blind Scouse, and either kind is eaten with red cabbage pickled in vinegar. However, like the years of poverty, Scouse is now part of Liverpool's history. Visitors to the city will search in vain for a restaurant that serves its own dish, although it is sometimes possible to find Irish stew (a direct ancestor) on bills of fare.

BEATLES BIRTHPLACES

George Harrison 12 Arnold Grove, Wavertree, 25 February 1943

John Lennon Oxford Street Maternity Hospital, 29 Oxford Street, Liverpool, 9 October 1940

Paul McCartney Aintree Hospital, 107 Rice Lane, Aintree, 18 June 1942

Ringo Starr 9 Madryn Street, Dingle, 7 July 1940

WELL, WELL, WELLS

With a population of just over 9,000, Wells (in Somerset) is the smallest cathedral city in England.

SHRINE TO THE METAL GURU

A plaque outside 25 Stoke Newington Common in north London commemorates the fact that T-Rex frontman Marc Bolan (born Marc Feld, on 30 September 1947, at nearby Hackney Hospital) was raised here. He died in 1977, after his Mini crashed into a tree on Barnes Common, and every year on the anniversary of his death hundreds of his fans lay flowers at the site.

CURRY: THE GREAT BRITISH DISH

Curry is now Britain's most popular meal. It became popular among the English living in India during the days of the British Empire. The word 'curry' comes from *kari*, meaning 'sauce', and grew out of a need to preserve meat in a hot climate.

PENNY LANE

Penny Lane no longer exists, but the barber, banker and 'shelter in the middle of a roundabout' can still be seen at the traffic junction of Smithdown Place. The barber's, Tony Slavin, stands on the curve of Cronton Road and Church Road; the bank is at the junction of Heathfield Road and Smithfield Road; while the shelter has been turned into a café.

APPLEBY HORSE FAIR

Appleby-in-Westmorland is the site of one of the most colourful and spectacular events in Britain. Since 1685 it has hosted the nation's largest horse fair every June. It attracts gypsies from all over the country, a gathering of horsemen, horse-drawn caravans and traditional gypsy skills and crafts.

THE FAB FOUR: SOME BREATHTAKING BEATLES FACTOIDS

Total weeks in the charts: 456
This total actually leaves The Beatles in seventh place. The top position is taken by Elvis, with an astounding 1,168 weeks in the charts.

Number Ones: 17
This tops the list of 'Most Number Ones by any single act', although unfortunately The Beatles tie with Elvis. Elvis had another Number One in 2002, taking his total to 18, but this was a DJ remix with his name sharing the track billing (Elvis vs JXL, 'A Little Less Conversation').

Consecutive Christmas Number Ones: 3
Again, this is a record, but again jointly held with The Spice Girls.

Consecutive Top 10 hits: 18
Top is Madonna (with 35), then it's Cliff Richard (21). Abba also had 18.

First British act to have a US Number One:
The first British Number One in the US was...not The Beatles – it was The Tornados, with 'Telstar'. The Beatles were second, with 'I Want To Hold Your Hand', more than a year later.

Largest single sale in one week: 970,000
This is the largest ever sale in one week by a non-charity single – 'I Want To Hold Your Hand'.

Largest advance sale of a single in one week: 1,400,000
This is the largest ever advance sale by a non-charity single – for 'Can't Buy Me Love'.

KARAOKE KING

Stockport, Lancashire, is the unlikely birthplace of what has become the bane of many a night down the pub. In 1975, local inventor Roy Brooke created 'Roy's Singalong Machine', which allowed singers to read song lyrics while an instrumental version of the song played in the background. The invention was bought by a Japanese company, who renamed it *karaoke* (literally 'empty orchestra'). It became an immediate hit in bars throughout Japan, before it was re-exported back to the UK and around the world. Thanks, Roy...

ON THE NOSE

The first Grand National, then called the Grand Liverpool Steeplechase, took place in 1839.

MIND YOUR LANGUAGE IN LONDON

There are an incredible 147 languages spoken within the area made up by the Inner London Education Authority (ILEA). In descending order, the 12 most spoken are:

English • Bengali • Turkish • Gujarati • Spanish • Greek • Urdu • Punjabi • Chinese • Italian • Arabic • French

THE ROODEE

Chester was the site of Britain's first official horse race. It took place on the Roodee, an old Roman site used for training troops and playing sports. In 1540, the town elders were so concerned about the violent 300-a-side games of football being played there that they banned them and replaced them with horse racing.

A CHAMPION CHIPPIE

Harry Ramsden opened his first fish and chip shop in 1928, at White Cross, Guiseley, West Yorkshire. With its no-nonsense menu of fish, chips, mushy peas, bread and butter, and tea, the popularity of the shop grew and grew. It is now, indisputably, the world's largest chippie. Still on the same site as the original shop, it now employs 140 staff, who serve 234 tonnes (258 tons) of fish and 362 tonnes (400 tons) of chips to over a million customers every year.

START OF LEGEND

Billy Butlin opened his first Butlins Holiday Camp in Skegness in 1937.

SWEET-TOOTHED BRITS

The English buy one third of the world's production of boiled sweets.

BEER MONSTERS

More than 15.3 million litres (27 million pints) of beer are sold in the UK every day.

WHY THE SHAMROCK?

St Patrick found that the pagan Irish had great difficulty comprehending the doctrine of the Trinity. He held up a shamrock (similar to a three-leaf clover) to show how the three leaves combined to make a single plant, just as the Father, Son and Holy Ghost combined to make the Holy Trinity. The Irish understood at once, and from that time the shamrock has been the symbol of the land. Irishmen wear it in their hats on the saint's day.

BRITAIN'S HIGHEST PUB

Tarn Hill Inn, North Yorkshire, is situated 528m (1,723ft) above sea level.

CUTHBERT'S RESTLESS BONES

St Cuthbert decided to turn his back on the hurly-burly of the Dark Ages, and in AD 664 became a hermit on the remote Farne Islands off the Northumbrian Coast. He lived there alone until his death, in 687. A year later, monks came to the islands to remove his remains and take them to a specially prepared spot on nearby Lindisfarne. To their astonishment they found that after 11 years his body had not decayed. To avoid them being destroyed by Viking raiders, the monks carried Cuthbert's corpse around Northumberland for 100 years, until it was finally laid to rest in Durham Cathedral.

PROSTITUTES

The amount spent on prostitutes in the UK each year is £440 million ($730 million).

SPAGHETTI ON THE MENU

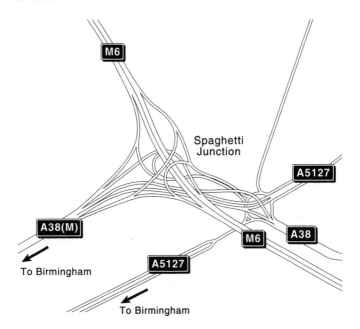

Spaghetti Junction is one of the most famous landmarks in the UK. On a road map it can be identified as Junction 6 on the M6 leading to the centre of Birmingham, but officially it is recorded as Gravelly Hill Interchange. Nobody ever uses this title, however, as 'Spaghetti Junction' perfectly captures both the essence of its appearance and travellers' experiences. The name almost allows people to visualise the way three motorways meet and tangle with a whole host of major and minor roads leading into and out of Birmingham. Raised hundreds of metres above the ground on concrete pillars, strips of road twist above, below and around each other, rather 'like an octopus trying to swat a fly'.

'ALL THE PEOPLE, SO MANY PEOPLE...': BRITAIN'S POPULATION

In July 2003, the number of people living in Britain was a grand 60,094,648. Population density in England is higher than the rest of Great Britain, with 375 people per square kilometre (971 per square mile).

A SELECTION OF HAUNTED HOUSES

Athelhampton Hall
Location: near Puddletown, Dorset
Origin: 16th century
Story: The lovelorn daughter of the Martyn family took her own life in a secret room in the house. Unfortunately, she locked in the family's pet monkey, who starved to death. The ape's ghostly scratching can still be heard on the wooden panelling.

Bosworth Hall
Location: Market Bosworth, Leicestershire
Origin: 1758
Story: The owner, Sir Wolston Dixie, discovered his daughter Ann was having an affair with the gardener. Horrified, he installed man traps around the house. Unfortunately, Ann stood in one and bled to death from her horrific injuries. Her ghost now stalks the house in search of her true love.

Bramshill House
Location: near Hartley Wintney, Hampshire
Origin: 18th century
Story: Sir John Cope's son, William, was celebrating his wedding day with a boisterous game of hide-and-seek. Sadly he proved far too good and suffocated after locking himself in a chest. His ghost now wanders the house, crying out for someone to find him.

Burton Agnes Hall
Location: near Bridlington, Humberside
Origin: early 17th century
Story: Anne, the youngest daughter of owner Sir Henry Griffiths, was attacked and killed by two beggars. Her dying wish was that her skull be kept in the house, which she had always loved. Her family thought she was joking, but they soon changed their mind when – having buried her remains complete – they were subjected to a barrage of ghostly banging. This only ceased when the skull was brought into the house, where it is supposedly hidden to this day.

Courtier's House
Location: Clifton Hampden, near Oxford.
Origin: 18th century
Story: In 1799, Sarah Fletcher, the wife of a sea captain, hanged herself in her bedroom after discovering her husband was engaged in a bigamous marriage. She was buried in Dorchester Abbey, but she continues to haunt her old home in a black cloak and purple ribbon.

Ightham Mote

Location: near Sevenoaks, Kent

Origin: 17th century

Story: On 5 November 1605, house owner Dame Dorothy Selby sent a note to Lord Montague, warning him not to attend Parliament that day. Her actions led to the discovery of the Gunpowder Plot. Those conspirators who escaped wreaked revenge on Dame Dorothy by locking her in a secret room in the house to die. Her bones were discovered more than 300 years later, and ever since she has haunted the house.

Penfound Manor

Location: near Poundstock, Cornwall

Origin: 17th century

Story: Young Kate Penfound was in love with John Trebarnfoot and wanted to marry him. The trouble was, this was the time of the English Civil War and, while John was a staunch Parliamentarian, Kate's father was a fervent Royalist. One day he caught the pair trying to elope, and in the ensuing fight John was killed, while Kate and her father were mortally wounded. Kate still stalks the house looking for her lost love, while on 26 April (the anniversary of the fateful day) all three spooks can be seen together.

Pythouse

Location: Semley, Wiltshire

Origin: Unknown

Story: The Bennett-Stanfords have lived in this house for more than 700 years, but some time in the 16th century their housemaid Polly accidentally scalded her child's feet. The child died and Polly was hanged – only to return in ghostly guise, wailing about the loss of her precious baby.

KIELDER WATER

Kielder Water in Northumberland is the largest man-made lake in Europe. Completed in 1980, it was created by damming and flooding the North Tyne Valley. It took a year and a half to fill, which is hardly surprising, given that it contains 200 billion litres (53 billion gallons) of water, has a perimeter of 43km (27 miles) and a surface area of 10.9 sq km (4.1 sq miles). The supply tunnel from the lake's pumping station to Eggleston on the Tees is 30.6km (19 miles) – the longest in Britain. If that isn't enough, the lake stands in the middle of Kielder Forest, not only the largest forest in Britain but also the largest artificially planted forest in Europe, covering an area of 393.7 sq km (152 sq miles).

SOME FASCINATING FACTS ABOUT LIVERPOOL

10 million day-trippers visit Liverpool every year.

Visitors to Liverpool spend £600 million ($1 billion) every year in the city.

A £14 million ($23 million) millennium project in St Helens has created a world-class interactive tourist attraction. World Of Glass opened in 2000 and celebrated the region's influence in glassmaking.

Liverpool has been awarded the prestigious accolade of European City of Culture for 2008.

The Albert Dock is one of the UK's biggest tourist attractions, with over 5 million visitors per year.

Merseyside has almost 50km (30 miles) of beaches – more than any other urban area in Britain.

Britain's first ever package holiday flight flew from Liverpool Airport to the south of France in 1952. The first scheduled flight from a regional airport was from Liverpool to Amsterdam in 1934.

Liverpool was voted 'Day Trip Destination 1998' by the English Tourist Board.

The famous Mersey Ferries have been taking people across the Mersey, between Liverpool and the Wirral, for 870 years.

There are five Mersey Ferries – *The Royal Daffodil*, *Mountwood*, *Overchurch*, *Woodchurch* and the recently refurbished *Royal Iris*. Each is 46m (152ft) long and weighs 472 tonnes (520 tons).

BRAINS OF BRITAIN

Average IQ of the population in major UK cities
107 points: Londonderry
105 points: Aberdeen, Bristol, Leeds, Leicester, London, Norwich, Southampton
104 points: Aberystwyth, Brighton, Liverpool, Manchester, Newcastle
103 points: Birmingham, Glasgow, Plymouth.
(The national IQ average is 100.)

WAKEMAN (RIPON, NOT RICK)

Visitors to Ripon are often startled to see a man blowing a horn in the town square at 9pm. This 1,000-year-old ceremony is known as Setting the Watch and signifies that the horn-blower – the Ripon Wakeman – is taking care of their city for the night.

THE BERWICK PROBLEM

Is it English or Scottish? This is the conundrum that has dominated the border town of Berwick-upon-Tweed. The Tweed forms the boundary of England and Scotland, and ownership of Berwick changed no less than 14 times between the 12th and 15th centuries. In 1482, it fell under English control and has remained there ever since, although Berwick Rangers football team still plays in the Scottish league.

BRITAIN'S TOP VISITOR ATTRACTIONS (PAID)

Attraction	Location	Visitors in 2002
British Airways London Eye	London	4,090,000
Tower of London	London	1,940,856
Eden Project	St Austell	Around 1,832,482
Legoland Windsor	Windsor	1,453,000
Flamingo Land Theme Park and Zoo	Kirby Misperton	Around 1,393,300
Windermere Lake Cruises	Ambleside	1,266,027
Drayton Manor Family Theme Park	Tamworth	Around 1,200,000
Edinburgh Castle	Edinburgh	1,153,317
Chester Zoo	Chester	1,134,949
Canterbury Cathedral	Canterbury	Around 1,110,529
Westminster Abbey	London	1,058,854
Kew Gardens	Richmond	969,188
Windsor Castle	Windsor	931,042
London Zoo	London	891,028
Roman Baths	Bath	845,608
New MetroLand	Gateshead Metro Centre	Around 810,000
Royal Academy of Arts	London	794,042
St Paul's Cathedral	London	781,364
Stonehenge	Amesbury	759,697
The Deep	Hull	Around 750,000

STARS WHO HAVE APPEARED IN CORONATION STREET

Pete Postlethwaite, Prince Charles, Paula Wilcox, Patricia Routledge, Prunella Scales, Paul Shane, Martin Shaw, Max Wall, Joanne Whalley, Kevin Whately, Peter Noone, Bill Owen, Trevor MacDonald, Bill Maynard, Fulton Mackay, Ben Kingsley, Sam Kelly, John Junkin, Sue Johnston, Davy Jones, Noddy Holder, Tim Healy, Michael Crawford, June Brown, Anthony Booth, Richard Beckinsale.

THE ORIGIN OF 'GEORDIE'

The most attractive historical explanation for why Newcastle people are called 'Geordies' takes us back to the 18th century and the time of the first Jacobite rising (in 1715). Newcastle's trade and livelihood depended so much on royal approval that its merchants and gentry could not risk becoming involved in a plot against George I. There were some Jacobite sympathisers in the town, especially among the working classes, but officially the Newcastle folk had to declare for King 'Geordie'. Newcastle's standing as a supporter of King Geordie angered the Jacobites, who may well have given the Newcastle people their famous nickname.

TOP 10 HOUSES AND HISTORIC MONUMENTS

Tower of London

Windsor Castle

Edinburgh Castle

Roman Baths and Pump Room

Stonehenge

Warwick Castle

Hampton Court Palace

Leeds Castle, Kent

Shakespeare's Birthplace, Stratford-upon-Avon

Blenheim Palace

THE LONG AND WINDING ROAD

At over 640km (400 miles), the A1 is Britain's longest A road, more than 160km (100 miles) longer than its nearest rival, the A38. The A1 has primary status between the Inner London Ring Road (A501) at the Angel and the Edinburgh City Bypass (A720). It has no fewer than six separate motorway sections (Hertfordshire, Cambridgeshire, South Yorkshire, West Yorkshire, North Yorkshire and Durham).

BUCK HOUSE WAS A SNIP

Buckingham Palace was purchased by George III in 1762 for the princely sum of £21,000 ($35,000).

DARE YOU RISK THE DEEP?

The Deep in Hull is the world's only submarium, and also the world's deepest aquarium, containing 5 million litres (1.3 million gallons) of water and 87 tonnes (96 tons) of salt. Visitors descend into the depths in a glass elevator that is often buzzed by sharks.

THE MIDLANDS' TOP VISITOR ATTRACTIONS (FREE)

Attraction	Location	Visitors in 2002
Carsington Water Visitor Centre	Ashbourne	Around 800,000
Wicksteed Park	Kettering	Around 500,000
Birmingham Museum and Art Gallery	Birmingham	427,288
Gloucester Cathedral	Gloucester	Around 330,000
Jinney Ring Craft Centre	Hanbury	Around 300,000
Linacre Reservoirs	Cutthorpe	Around 250,000
Coventry Cathedral	Coventry	Around 250,000
Ye Olde Pork Pie Shoppe	Melton Mowbray	231,777

BRITAIN'S WORLD BEATERS

Largest Norman crypt:	Canterbury Cathedral, Kent
Heaviest peal of bells:	Liverpool Cathedral
Oldest Methodist chapel:	New Room, Bristol
Largest inhabited castle:	Windsor Castle
Oldest Carnegie library:	Dunfermline, Scotland
Largest arts festival:	Edinburgh Festival
Smallest barber shop:	Brighton Pier
Oldest model village:	Bekonscot, Beaconsfield, Bucks
Largest camera obscura:	Aberystwyth, Wales
Oldest public zoo:	The Zoological Society, London
Oldest pot plant:	Kew Gardens
Oldest licensed brewery:	Bushmills, Northern Ireland
Largest turkey farm:	Bernard Matthews, Norfolk
Longest suspension bridge:	Humber Road Bridge
Largest illuminated bridge:	Forth Rail Bridge
First iron bridge:	Ironbridge, Telford
First railway station:	Liverpool Road Station, Manchester
Oldest passenger railway coaches:	Talyllyn Railway, Wales
First underground railway:	London Underground
Oldest commissioned ship:	HMS *Victory*, Portsmouth
Oldest iron-hulled warship:	HMS *Warrior*, Portsmouth
Oldest iron-hulled, screw-driven ship:	SS *Great Britain*, Bristol
Busiest international airport:	Heathrow
Largest moveable barrier:	Thames Barrier
Largest brickworks:	London Brick Company, Bedfordshire
Longest shopping mall:	Milton Keynes
Largest toyshop:	Hamleys, London
Largest bookshop:	Foyles, London
Largest fish and chip shop:	Harry Ramsden's

WATERLOO STORY

Waterloo train station is where, according to The Kinks' hit 'Waterloo Sunset', 'Terry' meets 'Julie'. It is rumoured that 'Terry' was the actor Terence Stamp, while 'Julie' was actress Julie Christie. Both were celluloid heartthrobs who had just appeared in the John Schlesinger movie *Far From The Madding Crowd*. The clock at Waterloo station is a famous rendezvous point for blind dates.

TOP 10 MOST-VISITED ATTRACTIONS (FREE)

Blackpool Pleasure Beach

Liverpool Albert Docks

British Museum

Strathclyde Park

National Gallery

Brighton Pier

Westminster Abbey

Yarmouth Pleasure Beach

St Paul's Cathedral

York Minster

THANK YOU VERY MUCH: THE KING IN THE UK

It's often said that Elvis Presley never visited the UK. Well he did –
albeit for a few minutes, when his plane landed at Prestwick Airport near
Glasgow for refuelling on its way back to the USA on 2 March 1960.
Presley was on his way home from a stint in the army in Germany,
and gamely stepped out to stretch his legs and meet a few fans at
the perimeter fence before he hopped back on board and continued
his journey.

HOW DID BIG BEN GET ITS NAME

Big Ben is the name given to the Great Bell – it weighs 13.8 tonnes (15.2
tons) – in the clock tower of the Palace of Westminster. There are two
theories of how the bell got its name. The first suggests that it was taken
from the nickname of a champion heavyweight boxer of the time called Ben
Caunt. The second (and more probable) explanation is that it was named
after the bulky Welshman Sir Benjamin Hall, who was First Commissioner
of Works from 1855 to 1858 and whose name was inscribed on the bell.

LB OR POUNDS?

The shorthand for the imperial measurement 'pound' is 'lb'. This is
an abbreviation of 'libra', the star sign whose symbol is a pair of
weighing scales.

BURIED WITH HONOURS

The number of persons buried in the church and cloisters of Westminster Abbey is estimated to be approximately 3,300. Proper registers were not kept until 1607, but existing monuments and medieval tomb lists provide the names of many more. This number does not include the many monks who were buried in a special cemetery behind the chapterhouse.

The Dean of Westminster must give his permission for all burials and monuments in the church. Ashes only are permitted. People who have served the Abbey in an official capacity, such as a dean, a canon, organist or surveyor of the fabric may be buried here, and eminent persons of British nationality from various fields may be considered. The last poet interred was John Masefield in 1967, and the actor/director Laurence Olivier was buried here in 1989.

Among those buried at Westminster Abbey are:

Geoffrey Chaucer, poet	died 1400
Anne of Cleves	died 1557
Mary Queen of Scots	died 1587
Oliver Cromwell	died 1658
Isaac Newton, scientist	died 1727
George Frederic Handel, composer	died 1759
William Pitt (the Younger), prime minister	died 1806
Viscount Palmerston, prime minister	died 1865
Charles Dickens, novelist	died 1870
David Livingstone, explorer	died 1873
Charles Darwin, naturalist	died 1882
William Ewart Gladstone, prime minister	died 1888
Robert Browning, poet	died 1889
Alfred Tennyson, poet	died 1892
Thomas Hardy, novelist	died 1928
Rudyard Kipling, writer	died 1936
Neville Chamberlain, prime minister	died 1940
Ralph Vaughan Williams, composer	died 1958
Clement Attlee, prime minister	died 1967
Lawrence Olivier, actor	died 1989

LONDON PARKLIFE

London might have a reputation these days as being one huge traffic jam exuding smoke and fumes by the lungful, but the capital boasts an impressive 1,800 parks, gardens and open spaces.

THE WORDS TO 'FLOWER OF SCOTLAND'

O Flower of Scotland,
When will we see your like again
That fought and died for
Your wee bit hill and glen.
And stood against him,
Proud Edward's army,
And sent him homeward
Tae think again.

The hills are bare now,
And autumn leaves lie thick and still
O'er land that is lost now,
Which those so dearly held.
That stood against him,
Proud Edward's army,
And sent him homeward
Tae think again.

Those days are past now
And in the past they must remain,
But we can still rise now
And be the nation again!
That stood against him,
Proud Edward's army,
And sent him homeward
Tae think again.

O Flower of Scotland,
When will we see your like again
That fought and died for
Your wee bit hill and glen.
And stood against him,
Proud Edward's army,
And sent him homeward
Tae think again.

UP AND DOWN

The shortest scheduled airline flight in the UK is made between the islands of Westray and Papa Westray. The flight lasts two minutes.

SOME MORE UNFORTUNATE PLACE NAMES

Bonkle, Lanarkshire

Bottoms, West Yorkshire

Catbrain, Avon

Lower Assenden, Oxfordshire

North Piddle, Worcestershire

Ogle, Northumberland

Pant, Shropshire

Pratt's Bottom, Kent

Slaggyford, Northumberland

Twatt, Orkney

Undy, Gwent

FORTH RAIL BRIDGE

Until 1890, getting north from Edinburgh involved a lengthy detour along the Firth of Forth. In 1892, however, work commenced on the Forth Rail Bridge, one of the most spectacular feats of Victorian engineering. The complete bridge carries a double railway track over the Forth, 47.5m (156ft) above the water level. At 521m (1,710ft) long, it is the longest cantilever bridge in Britain, and the second longest in the world.

It was designed by Sir John Fowler and Sir Benjamin Baker, and around 5,000 men were employed to build it. The builders described it as 'the workman's bridge', as it was the workmen themselves who had to use their own skills and initiative to overcome the hundreds of unseen difficulties arising in this scale of construction. On completion, one of the engineers, when asked how long the bridge would last, replied, 'For ever if you look after it.' Since then the bridge has employed a full-time painting squad, who have painted it continuously, but this has been stepped down in recent years, prompting fears in some quarters that the bridge is in decline.

MONEY FOR OLD ROPE?

British Members of Parliament get paid £56,358 ($93,554) a year to represent their constituents in the House of Commons.

SOME FACTS ABOUT TOURISM

24 per cent of all leisure day visits in 1998 were to the countryside.

Visits to the countryside accounted for 25 per cent of total domestic tourism in England in 1999.

Tourists visiting the English countryside tend to be aged 25 to 54.

85 per cent of the 24.7 million tourist trips made to the countryside in 1999 were made by car, 5 per cent were made by train, and 2 per cent by public bus or coach.

In the UK, tourism generates £8 billion ($13 billion) a year and accounts for 4 per cent of Gross Domestic Product and 1.5 million jobs.

Blackpool, Lancashire, attracts nearly 17 million visitors a year, with an annual expenditure of £545 million ($900 million).

UK tourism supports 1.7 million jobs directly or indirectly.

BRITAIN – THE BEST IN EUROPE

Largest man-made lake:	Kielder Water (by volume), Rutland Water (by area)
Largest man-made forest:	Kielder Forest
Largest artifical mound:	Silbury Hill, Wiltshire
Largest hill fort:	Maiden Castle, Dorset
Oldest inhabited street:	Vicar's Close, Wells, Somerset
Largest Chinese gateway:	Imperial Arch, Manchester
Largest crypt:	St Paul's
Largest organ:	Liverpool Cathedral
Oldest book room:	Winchester Cathedral
Largest chained library:	Hereford Cathedral
Largest public reference library:	The Mitchell Library, Glasgow
Largest indoor theme park:	Gateshead Metroland
Largest TV theme park:	Granada Studio tours, Manchester
Largest man-made marina:	Brighton
Longest rail tunnel:	Channel Tunnel, Folkestone, Kent
Longest cantilever bridge:	Forth Rail Bridge
Longest cable-stayed bridge:	Queen Elizabeth Bridge, Dartford–Tilbury
Deepest road cutting:	M62 at Dean Head
Largest cranes:	Goliath and Samson, Harland and Wolff Shipyard, Belfast

SANDWICH FILLER

The word 'sandwich' was born in London one very late night in 1762, when an English nobleman, John Montagu, the Fourth Earl of Sandwich (1718–92), was too busy gambling to stop for a meal, even though he was hungry for some food. The legend goes that he ordered a waiter to bring him roast beef between two slices of bread (apparently, the meat was to be put on slices of bread so he wouldn't get his fingers greasy while playing cards). The earl was therefore able to continue his gambling while eating his snack, and from that incident we have inherited that quick-food product that we now know as the humble (yet magnificent) sandwich.

THE REAL ST GEORGE

St George was born in Cappadocia (now in eastern Turkey) in AD 270, and at the age of 17 joined the Roman army and soon became renowned for his bravery.

Though he served under a pagan emperor, he never forgot his Christian faith. Emperor Diocletian gave him many important missions, and it is thought that on one of these he came to England. While he was in Britain, he heard that the emperor was putting all Christians to death, so George returned to Rome to help his brother Christians. He pleaded with the Emperor to spare their lives, but Diocletian did all he could to persuade St George to give up his faith. George refused, however, and was finally beheaded on 23 April 303.

Around 1,000 years later, St George became England's patron saint (replacing Edward the Confessor), and 23 April was made a national feast day in 1415.

St George is also patron saint of soldiers, archers, cavalry and chivalry, farmers and field workers, riders and saddlers, and he helps those suffering from leprosy, plague and syphilis.

LET THERE BE LIGHT

The Savoy Theatre became the first theatre to be lit by electricity – in 1881.

OUGH

The syllable -*ough* can be pronounced eight different ways ('oh', 'or', 'ow', 'oo', 'er', 'uff', 'off' and 'up'). The following sentence contains them all:

'A dough-faced, thoughtful ploughman strode through the streets of Scarborough; after falling into a slough, he coughed and hiccoughed.'

UK MARRIAGES AND DIVORCES IN 1999

	Marriages	Divorces
England	249,490	137,154
Wales	14,025	7,402
Scotland	29,940	11,864
Northern Ireland	7,628	2,326

FASCINATING FACTS ABOUT ST KILDA

St Kilda is Europe's most important seabird colony, and one of the major seabird breeding stations in the North Atlantic.

The world's largest colony of gannets nests on Boreray and the sea stacs.

St Kilda has the largest colony of fulmars in the British Isles – nearly 65,000 in 1999.

Seabirds formed a major part of the St Kildan diet, especially gannets, fulmars and puffins. At one time it was estimated that each person on St Kilda ate 115 fulmars every year. In 1876, it was said that the islanders took 89,600 puffins for food and feathers.

The St Kildans used to eat puffins for a snack – just like a packet of crisps!

Stac an Armin (191m/627ft) and Stac Lee (165m/541ft) are the highest sea stacs in Britain.

St Kilda is one of the best places in Britain for diving, because of its clear water and its submerged caves, tunnels and arches.

In the 1850s, 42 islanders emigrated to Australia. Many of them died en route, but a few settled in Melbourne, and to this day a suburb of the Australian city is called St Kilda (named after the schooner *The Lady Of St Kilda*, which was anchored off the shore at around this time). There is also a St Kilda in New Zealand.

BRITAIN'S FIRST ASTRONAUT IN SPACE

In 1989, Helen Sharman, an engineer with the Mars confectionery company, was selected as a commercial astronaut. Her flight with the USSR was funded by companies in the UK. On 18 May 1991, the Soyuz spacecraft carrying the 'Juno' mission took off from the Baikonur Cosmodrome. In all, Sharman spent about eight days in space, including the flights to and from the Mir Space Station. After the flight she became a spokesperson for science and technology in Britain, and has presented a science programme on BBC Radio 4. Sharman is still the only British citizen to have flown in space, but she is backing the proposal to put a Brit on the International Space Station.

IF ONLY THEY COULD SPELL!

Covent Garden is really a spelling mistake! The area used to be the market garden for what is now Westminster Abbey monastery and convent.

BOTTOMS UP! CHIN-CHIN!

In the average British restaurant, you will eat 27p (45c) worth of food for every £1 ($1.70) you spend.

The average 10-year-old British kid eats his or her own weight in chips every nine months.

On average, Brits throw away 44,000 tonnes (49,000 tons) of food a day.

The most popular craving for pregnant British women is curry.

Brits eat more than 225g (8oz) of cheese per person every week.

The percentage of tea in British people's fluid intake is 42 per cent.

At any one time, 0.7 per cent of Brits are drunk.

A total of 6.7 billion litres (11.8 billion pints) of beer are drunk in Britain every year.

If all the cans of Spam ever eaten in Britain were put end to end, they would circle the globe at least ten times.

Over 60,000 British people end up hospitalised every year with an injury caused by opening a packet of food.

WHAT IS AN ARMY?

A modern definition is an organised body of men armed for war, but the Laws of King Ine of Wessex (688–728) were quite specific:

Up to 7 men = Thieves
7–35 men = a Band
35+ men = an Army

INVASION!

On 22 February 1797, an Irish-American revolutionary called General William Tate led a force of 1,200 French soldiers ashore at Carregwastad Point near Fishguard. His plan was simple: invade Britain and overthrow George III. Sadly, Tate's invasion lasted less than two days before they were captured by local townsfolk. Legend has it that the French saw the Welsh women dressed in traditional costume and flung down their arms because, from a distance, they thought they were being surrounded by British Redcoats. Tate's abortive mission was the last invasion of Britain.

ENGLAND VS SCOTLAND: BATTLES SINCE 1066

Date	Place	Region	Result
1136	Carlisle	Cumberland	Scots defeated English
1174	Alnwick	Northumberland	English defeated Scots
1296	Loudon Hill	Darvell, Ayrs	Wallace defeated English
1296	Berwick	Northumberland	Edward I defeated Scottish nobles
1297	Sanquhar	Dumfries	Sir William Douglas defeated English
1297	Dalswinton	Dumfries	William Wallace defeated English
1297	Stirling Bridge	Stirling	William Wallace defeated Earl of Surrey
1298	Falkirk	Stirlingshire	Edward I defeated William Wallace
1303	Stirling	Stirlingshire	Edward I defeated Scots
1304	Happrew	Lauder, Midlothian	Edward I defeated William Wallace
1307	Sanquhar	Dumfries	Sir James (The Black) Douglas defeated English
1307	Paisley Forest	Renfrewshire	English defeated Scots
1311	Berwick	Northumberland	English defeated Robert Bruce
1311	Linlithgow	West Lothian	Robert Bruce defeated English
1312	Hexham	Northumberland	Robert Bruce defeated English
1312	Durham	Durham	Robert Bruce defeated English
1314	Bannockburn	Stirlingshire	Robert Bruce defeated Edward II
1318	Berwick	Northumberland	Robert Bruce defeated Edward II
1347	Roxburgh	Roxburgh	English defeated Scots
1380	Solway	English/Scottish border	Scots defeated English
1402	Nesbit Moor	Wooler, Northumberland	English defeated Scots
1460	Roxburgh	Roxburgh	Scots defeated English
1513	Norham	Northumberland	James IV, King of Scotland defeated English

1513 Flodden	Branxton, Northumberland	Earl of Surrey defeated James IV, King of Scotland
1746 Falkirk	Stirlingshire	Prince Charles Edward Stuart and Lord George Murray defeated Lt Gen Henry Hawley
1746 Culloden	Inverness	Duke of Cumberland defeated Prince Charles Edward Stuart
Final score:	**England 11, Scotland 15**	

AN ENGLISHMAN, IRISHMAN, SCOTSMAN JOKE

Despite existing as a unified nation, the presumed differences between the various countries in the UK have always been a source of great humour – and no more so than in the Englishman, Irishman, Scotsman jokes. (For some reason, the Welsh have always been exempt…)

A typical example is as follows:

There's an Englishman, Irishman and a Scotsman who work on a building site.

It's time for their dinner, so they sit down. The Englishman opens up his lunchbox and says, 'If I get cheese sandwiches tomorrow, I'm gonna throw myself off that bridge.' The Scotsman and Irishman say the same.

The next day, the Englishman has cheese sandwiches, so he jumps off the bridge. The Irishman and the Scotsman also have cheese in their sandwiches, so they, too, jump off the bridge.

At their joint funeral, the three wives meet up.

The Englishman's wife says, 'He should have said something. I could have given him a different filling.'

The Scotsman's wife agrees. 'Yes, I'd have made him something else instead.'

The Irishman's wife says, 'I don't understand why he jumped, because every morning he made his own sandwiches!'

UK'S WOODLAND

Woodland covers an estimated 2.7 million hectares (7 million acres) in the UK – a little less than 8 per cent of England, nearly 17 per cent of Scotland, 14 per cent of Wales and 6 per cent of Northern Ireland.

BRITISH POLITICAL PARTIES

Alliance Party of Northern Ireland
British Centre Party
British National Party
Central Alliance Party
Communist Party of Britain
Conservative Party
Green Party of England and Wales
Green Party of Northern Ireland
Highlands and Islands Alliance
Irish Republican Socialist Party
Labour Party
Legalise Cannabis Alliance
Liberal Democrats
Liberal Party
National Democrats
Natural Law Party
Northern Ireland Unionist Party
Official Monster Raving Loony Party
Plaid Cymru
Progressive Democratic Party
Progressive Unionist Party
Revolutionary Communist Party of Great Britain
Scottish Green Party
Scottish Liberal Democrats
Scottish National Party
Scottish Socialist Party
Sinn Fein
Social Democratic and Labour Party
Socialist Equality Party
Socialist Labour Party
Socialist Party
Socialist Party of Great Britain
Socialist Workers' Party
Socialist Workers' Party, Ireland
Socialist Workers' Party in Northern Ireland
Third Way
UK Independence Party
UK Pensioners' Party
Ulster Democratic Unionist Party
Ulster Third Way
Ulster Unionist Party
United Kingdom Unionist Party
Welsh Liberal Democrats

COCK FIGHTING

Cock fighting, for all its barbarity, was not outlawed in Britain until 1849. The most spectacular cockpit was a six-sided affair. Built in Welshpool in the early 1700s, it could accommodate more than 200 spectators.

AVERAGE AGE AT FIRST MARRIAGE IN ENGLAND AND WALES

Year	Male	Female
1969	25	22
1979	25	23
1989	27	25
1999	30	28

UK PILL POPPERS

UK pharmaceutical companies make three of the world's bestselling medicines:

Zantac (Glaxo Wellcome), for ulcer treatment
Tenormin (ICI), a beta-blocker for high blood pressure
AZT (Glaxo Wellcome), a drug used in the treatment of AIDs.

WHAT THE DICKENS?

Charles Dickens lived in Rochester and the surrounding area for most of his life. Local legend has it that his ghost is often seen wandering the High Street.

BRITAIN'S SHORTEST WAR

The shortest war in the world occurred between Britain and Zanzibar, and lasted for just 38 minutes. On 25 August 1896, the ruling Sultan Hamid bin Thuwain died. Two hours later, a usurper broke into the palace and declared himself ruler. (England was then the major superpower in the Indian Ocean and, since 1890, had established a protectorate on the island of Zanzibar.) The Royal Navy was asked to evict the usurper. On 27 August, three warships opened fire, and in little over half an hour they reduced the palace to rubble and deposed the usurper. The bombardment has since been credited as the shortest war in history.

ELEMENTARY

Fictional detective Sherlock Holmes lived at 221b Baker Street, London. The building is today occupied by the head office of the Abbey Building Society.

BRITAIN'S ODDEST PUB NAMES

The Hole In The Wall Dumfries

The Poosy Nancies Mauchline, Ayrshire (The Poosy Nancy was named after a female acquaintance of Robert Burns)

The Bucket Of Blood Cornwall

The Inn Next Door Burnt Down Bedfordshire

Mad Dog At Odell Odell, Bedfordshire

The Percy Hobbs Morn Hill, Hampshire (renamed in 1982 – from New Inn – in honour of a local man who had been drinking there since 1920)

The Sociable Plover Portsmouth

The Periscope Barrow-in-Furness

The Ibex West Berkshire

Tafarn Sinc Pembrokeshire (The Pub Made of Zinc, the highest pub in Pembrokeshire)

Chemic Tavern Woodhouse, Leeds

Alum House South Shields

Crown Posada Newcastle

Round Of Carrots Herefordshire

The Quiet Woman York (the sign being a woman carrying her own severed head)

The Old Thirteenth Cheshire Astley Volunteer Rifleman Corps Inn Stalybridge (longest pub name in the UK)

Q Stalybridge (shortest pub name in the UK; named after an earlier pub that closed in the 1930s)

Pipe And Gannex Huyton

Who'd A Thowt It Middleton

Sally Up Steps Bolton (originally called The Stanley Arms)

Bob's Smithy Bolton (named after the blacksmith who spent more time in the pub than he did at work)

The Lion Of Vienna Bolton (named after Nat Lofthouse of Bolton Wanderers Football Club and England)

The Strawbury Duck Entwistle

Oxnoble Manchester (named after a potato variety)

Peveril Of The Peak Castlefield, Manchester (named after a stagecoach that used to make the run from Manchester to London in only two days)

The Rain Bar Castlefield, Manchester (built in an old umbrella factory)

Cupid's Hill Inn Herefordshire

The Cat And Custard Pot Paddlesworth, Kent (formerly called The Cat And Mustard Pot)

The Rubayiat Of Omar Khayyam Glasgow

Muscular Arms Glasgow

Lass O' Gowrie Manchester
The Jabez Clegg Manchester
Hardy's Well Hardy's Well
The Thatcher's Foot County Durham
Cow And Snuffers Cardiff
The Jolly Taxpayer Plymouth
Donkey On Fire Ramsgate, Kent
The Adam And Eve Inn Paradise, Gloucestershire
Young Vanish Chesterfield (named after a racehorse)
Spinner And Bergamot Comberbach, Cheshire
Bull And Spectacles Staffordshire (used to be called the Bulls Head but
    many years ago, a drunken man climbed up the front of the pub and
    placed his glasses on the Bulls Head and left them there)
The Duke Without A Head Wateringbury, Kent
The Leg Of Mutton And Cauliflower London
World Turned Upside Down London
The Little B Brooklands, Manchester
Labouring Boys Isleworth, Middlesex
The Office Sheffield

MARYLEBONE MOP TOPS

During their film career, The Beatles kept returning to the area around
Marylebone Road for location shots. In the opening sequence of *A Hard
Day's Night*, the band run down Boston Place next to Marylebone station.
They then go into the station itself, where they are pursued by hundreds of
fans (who were paid for the privilege).

TOP 10 FIRST NAMES IN ENGLAND AND WALES

Girls	Boys
1. Chloe	1. Jack
2. Emily	2. Thomas
3. Megan	3. Joshua
4. Jessica	4. James
5. Sophie	5. Daniel
6. Lauren	6. Harry
7. Charlotte	7. Samuel
8. Hannah	8. Joseph
9. Olivia	9. Matthew
10. Lucy	10. Lewis

BRITAIN'S NATIONAL PARKS

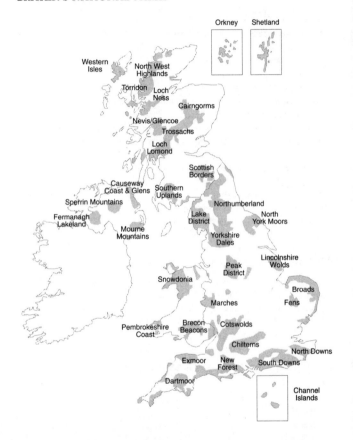

LIVERPOOL CATHEDRAL

Liverpool Cathedral is the largest in Britain – 190m (619ft) long, 54m (175ft) wide and 102m (331ft) tall. The foundation stone was laid by Edward VII in 1904, but it wasn't completed until 1978. Remarkably, the designer Giles Gilbert Scott was just 21 when he won a competition for its design. He would later design the unmistakable red telephone box.

EVERYTHING YOU EVER WANTED TO KNOW ABOUT BINGO

There are 688 licensed bingo clubs operating in the UK.

Figures for 2002 show an estimated total market of around 85 million admissions.

In 2002, £246 million ($408 million) was paid to the Exchequer in duty and VAT.

Estimated total industry pre-tax profit for 2002 was £149 million ($247 million).

The average customer spends £18–22 ($30–37) on a night at bingo (making no allowance for winnings). This includes bingo tickets, VAT and duty, other gaming, food and drink.

Over £999 million ($1.65 billion) was paid out in prizes in 2002 in licensed bingo clubs.

Bingo is the only gambling activity where women are more likely to play than men: 70 per cent of bingo players are women. Overall, 10 per cent of all women play, compared to only 5 per cent of men.

Bingo playing is spread evenly across all age categories, with the average age of players being under 50.

CUMBRIA'S TOP VISITOR ATTRACTIONS (PAID)

Attraction	Location	Visitors in 2002
Windermere Lake Cruises	Ambleside	1,266,027
Rheged: The Village in the Hill	Penrith	404,068
Tullie House Museum and Art Gallery	Carlisle	284,011
South Lakes Wild Animal Park	Dalton-in-Furness	Around 226,000
Aquarium of the Lakes	Newby Bridge	Around 200,000
Lakes Glass Centre	Ulverston	170,879
Lakeside and Haverthwaite Railway	Ulverston	Around 120,000
Ravenglass and Eskdale Railway	Ravenglass	Around 110,000

BRITAIN'S TRADE UNIONS

AMICUS (merger of Amalgamated Engineering and Electrical Union and Management, Science and Finance Union, January 2001)

Associated Society of Locomotive Engineers and Firemen

Association of Teachers and Lecturers

Association of University Teachers

Bakers', Food and Allied Workers' Union

British Air Line Pilots' Association

Broadcasting, Entertainment, Cinematograph and Theatre Union

Ceramic and Allied Trades Union

Communication Workers Union

Educational Institute of Scotland

Equity (actors)

FDA (senior civil servants)

Fire Brigades Union

GMB (general workers' union)

Graphical, Paper, and Media Union

Hospital Consultants and Specialists Association

Iron and Steel Trades Confederation

Musicians' Union

National Association of Probation Officers

National Association of Teachers in Further and Higher Education

National Union of Schoolmasters Union of Women Teachers

National Farmers Union

National Union of Journalists

National Union of Marine, Aviation and Shipping Transport Officers

National Union of Mineworkers

National Union of Rail, Maritime and Transport Workers

National Union of Students

National Union of Teachers

Prison Officers' Association

Public and Commercial Services Union

Professional Footballers Association

Prospect (engineering, scientific, management and professional staff)

Public and Commercial Services Union

Royal College of Nursing

Society of Chiropodists and Podiatrists

Society of Radiographers

Transport And General Workers' Union

Transport Salaried Staffs' Association

Undeb Cenedlaethol Athrawon Cymru (National Union of Teachers of Wales)

UNIFI (financial services)
Union of Construction, Allied Trades and Technicians
Union of Shop, Distributive and Allied Workers
Unison (Public services)
The Writers' Guild of Great Britain

FLASH HARRYS OF TUNBRIDGE WELLS

The lively social scene in Tunbridge Wells was famously organised by the dandy Richard Beau Nash, who divided his time between Tunbridge Wells and Bath. Nash made sure that residents and visitors alike adhered to the 'rules' of social behaviour.

PUNCHING BEYOND ITS WEIGHT

Despite having only one per cent of the world's population, Britain is the fifth largest trading nation in the world.

LOCATIONS FOR HARRY POTTER

Gloucester Cathedral provided the setting for the 'talking pictures' and ghost scenes, and the bathrooms that overflow in *Harry Potter And The Chamber Of Secrets*.

Oxford was the historic setting for Hogwarts' staircase, dining room, library and hospital. The staircase is featured in *The Chamber Of Secrets* – Professor Snape catches the children here on their late arrival back at school.

Alnwick Castle in Northumberland, ancestral home of the dukes of Northumberland, provided exterior shots of Hogwarts. The wonderful Quidditch match and the broomstick flying lessons were also filmed within the castle ramparts. A sign outside the castle recently read, 'The exterior of Hogwarts school'.

Goathland Station in North Yorkshire, built in 1865, was used as Hogsmead station. The North Yorkshire Moors Railway has featured in television programmes over the years, including *Brideshead Revisited* and *All Creatures Great And Small*.

Durham Cathedral, recently voted the best-loved building in Britain and described by Bill Bryson as 'the best Cathedral on planet earth', provided the setting for one of the classrooms, as well the memorable scene in which Harry walks through the cloisters with his owl, Hedwig.

THE ULTIMATE INSURANCE

In London around the year 1700, you could buy an insurance policy to protect you from going to hell.

BRITAIN'S HIGHEST MOUNTAINS

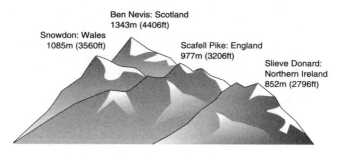

Ben Nevis: Scotland
1343m (4406ft)

Snowdon: Wales
1085m (3560ft)

Scafell Pike: England
977m (3206ft)

Slieve Donard:
Northern Ireland
852m (2796ft)

AHEAD OF THE TIMES?

Slavery was abolished in Britain's empire in 1833 – more than 30 years before it was outlawed in America.

POLITICAL CONSTITUENCIES

There are 659 political consitituencies in Britain (529 in England, 72 in Scotland, 40 in Wales, 18 in Northern Ireland).

The largest constituency (by electorate) is Isle of Wight, with 103,678 on the roll (in 1997).

The smallest constituency (by electorate) is the Western Isles, with 22,539 on the roll (in 1997).

The largest constituency (by area) is Ross, Skye and Inverness West, at a massive 918,319 hectares (371,644 acres).

The smallest constituency (by area) is the tiddly Islington North, at 727 hectares (292 acres).

HALLOWEEN HISTORY

Halloween started in 700 BC as a Druid festival called Samhain, which celebrated the death of summer and the start of the harvest.

A SELECTION OF ROYAL QUOTES

'I look upon him as the greatest criminal known for having plunged the world into this ghastly war.'
King George V, on cousin Wilhelm II, Kaiser of Germany

'Asking South American peasants to stop growing coca is like asking the Scots to stop growing barley because people on the other side of the world could not hold their drink.'
Princess Anne, on the drug battles with Colombia

Elizabeth (10) tells sister Margaret (6) that their Uncle Edward has abdicated:
Margaret: 'Does this mean you will be the next queen?'
Elizabeth: 'Yes, some day.'
Margaret: 'Poor you.'

'If people feel it has no further part to play, then for goodness' sakes let's end the thing on amicable terms without having a row about it.'
Prince Philip, referring to the monarchy's future role

'I will be good.'
Queen Victoria, as a child, learning that she will be queen one day

'I don't mind praying to the eternal father, but I must be the only man in the country afflicted with an eternal mother!'
Future King Edward VII, as Prince of Wales, waiting to succeed Queen Victoria

'A bloody awful mistake!'
Prince Charles commenting on his marriage

'I declare before you all that my whole life, whether it be long or short, shall be devoted to your service and to the service of our great Imperial Family to which we all belong.'
HM Queen Elizabeth II, as Princess Elizabeth

THE CURSE OF FLAT 12

Flat 12, 9 Curzon Place (near Hyde Park, London) is an unremarkable-looking apartment, yet it is the site of two famous rock 'n' roll deaths. On 29 July 1974, Mama Cass of The Mamas And The Papas expired after choking on a ham sandwich. Four years later, in the same flat, wild man Keith Moon, drummer with The Who, overdosed on pills that had been prescribed to cure his alcoholism.

BRITAIN IN RANDOM NUMBERS

14	per cent of Britons keep their New Year's Resolution.
26	per cent of British women are single.
34	per cent of British men are single.
50	average number of Christmas cards sent by Brits.
360	amount in pounds that Brits spend on Christmas presents each year ($600).
500	amount in pounds that Princess Anne was fined after becoming the first senior royal with a criminal record in November 2002, when her English bull terrier attacked two children ($830).
624	weekly salary in pounds for a London worker ($1,036), compared to £399 ($662) in the north .
2,000	cost in pounds of each outfit made for the Queen for her Golden Jubilee celebrations ($3,320).
27,000	kilos of strawberries consumed during Wimbledon fortnight (12,250lb).
50,000	tennis balls used during Wimbledon fortnight.
54,000	sprouts eaten each week by the residents of Diss, Norfolk.
270,000	heroin addicts in Britain.
1.1 million	Brits who give up smoking every year.
7.2 million	pounds spent on nicotine replacement aids for the 4 million smokers who attempt to give up every year ($12 million).

FRANK HOPE-JONES AND THE PIPS

Frank Hope-Jones was a well-known amateur radio enthusiast and horologist, and on 21 April 1923 he was giving a talk on BBC radio about summertime. As the talk finished, he counted aloud the last five seconds up to 10pm. After the broadcast, he suggested that maybe the BBC could have a more accurate time signal, using audible 'pips'. Frank Dyson (then Astronomer Royal) backed the idea, and the Royal Greenwich Observatory was approached to see if they could link this with their accurate timekeeping equipment. The equipment was designed so that a chronometer's escapement wheel at the observatory controlled a switch, which in turn controlled the output of a 1kHz oscillator. This generated six short pips (starting at five seconds to the hour and ending on the hour), which were then sent down a GPO line to the BBC for broadcast. These first pips were transmitted on 5 February 1924, and are still used to this day.

THE BLARNEY STONE

The Blarney Stone is believed to be half of the Stone of Scone, which originally belonged to Scotland. Scottish kings were crowned over the stone, because it was believed to have special powers. In 1314, the stone was given to Cormac McCarthy by Robert the Bruce, in return for his support in the Battle of Bannockburn. Queen Elizabeth I wanted Irish chiefs to agree to occupy their own lands under title from her. McCarthy, the Lord of Blarney, handled every royal request with subtle diplomacy, promising loyalty to the Queen without 'giving in'. Elizabeth, however, proclaimed that McCarthy was giving her 'a lot of Blarney', so giving rise to the legend – whoever kisses it is said to have been given the skill of flattery. You too can acquire this gift, by kissing the stone!

SOUTHERN INVASIONS

55 BC Julius Caesar's Roman Army, beaten back at Deal.

54 BC Julius Caesar again, reaches modern-day Brentford before retreating

AD 43 Plautius, the general of Emperor Claudius, lands at Hythe with 20,000 men. Within 40 years most of southern England is under Roman control.

AD 449 Abandoned by the Romans, Hengist and Horsa lead their Saxon hordes ashore at Pegwell Bay.

AD 597 St Augustine and 40 monks arrive at Pegwell Bay to bring Christianity to England.

AD 1066 William the Conqueror arrives and defeats King Harold at Senlac Hill near Hastings.

DOING TIME DOWN UNDER

Between 1788 and 1850, the English sent over 162,000 convicts to Australia in 806 ships. The first 11 of these ships are today known as the First Fleet, and contained the convicts and marines that are now acknowledged as the founders of Australia.

THE DOME: THE FACTS

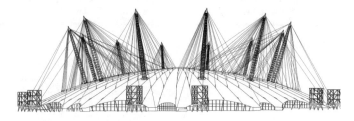

The Dome in Greenwich, London, is twice the size of the one in Atlanta, Georgia.

If you turned the Dome upside down and put it under Niagara Falls, it would take ten minutes to fill with water.

It is the largest fabric structure in the world, containing 93,000 sq m (1 million sq ft) of fabric.

In volume terms, it could hold as much water as 1,100 Olympic-size swimming pools or 2.2 billion litres (3.8 billion pints) of beer!

The roof of the Dome covers 80,000 sq m (20 acres) and is so strong it could support the weight of a jumbo jet.

The Dome is ten times the floor area of St Paul's Cathedral – you really could invite all your friends.

There are 70km (44 miles) of steel forming the 'cobweb' that supports the roof.

The Dome has lain unused since 2000.

TOP 10 PHOBIAS IN BRITAIN

1. Spiders
2. People and social situations
3. Flying
4. Open spaces
5. Confined spaces
6. Heights
7. Vomiting
8. Cancer
9. Thunderstorms
10. Death

A SELECTION OF ROYAL FACTOIDS

King Harold II, a former holder of the title Earl of Wessex, enjoyed a rapid rise to fame before his death at the Battle of Hastings in 1066. He inherited the title of Earl of Wessex from his father Godwin in 1053, having previously been the Earl of East Anglia.

Queen Victoria's best-known line, 'We are not amused', seems to fit well with all of the stern, unsmiling photos of her. But, there's no actual proof of her uttering this famous phrase. What she is known to have said was, 'I was very much amused.'

During the reign of Henry VII, Bristol was enormously rich thanks to the shipping of Cotswold wool, Iceland fish and Bordeaux wine. This is where the saying 'All shipshape and Bristol fashion' originated.

King Henry VII's wife, Elizabeth of York, is the queen depicted on playing cards, which were invented in 1486.

Queen Victoria is the longest reigning monarch in history. Ruling for a whopping 63 years, she passed away in 1901, aged 81.

The name 'England' comes from the tribes of people who settled there – the Angles, Saxons and Jutes, but most notably the Angles! 'England' evolved from 'Angle-land'.

Queen Elizabeth II has more British blood in her than most of her ancestors who were sovereigns. She has Scottish ancestry from her mother's side (indeed, the Queen Mother was descended from Scottish kings).

Heir presumptive is the title of a successor whose place in line may be bumped by the birth of another heir. However, an heir apparent cannot be bumped aside unless that heir decides to abdicate.

LA DOVER!

Dover is the nearest point in the UK to the Continent – the French coast is just 21 miles away. The famous white cliffs are 107m (350ft) high.

THE REAL OLDEST MAN IN BRITAIN

In a gravel pit at Boxgrove, just outside Chichester, the remains of a man were discovered that are thought to be half a million years old. Only a shinbone and two teeth were discovered, but his position (under thick layers of gravel) show that he is the oldest 'man' so far discovered in Britain.

GREAT ORME

Great Orme is a huge 207m- (678ft-) high rock, which dominates the skyline at Llandudno, in Wales. In the 19th century Llandudno was transformed from a dwindling mining community into a thriving seaside resort for holidaymakers from Lancashire and the Midlands. Ingenious methods were employed to get to Great Orme's summit, but in 1902 the Great Orme Tramway was opened – a 3ft 6in- (107cm-) gauge double tramway based on the San Francisco models. If that's not to your liking, there is always the Llandudno Chairlift, Britain's longest cable car, which measures a whopping 1622m (5320ft).

THE REAL ST PATRICK

St Patrick was born in either Scotland or Wales, the son of Roman parents living in Britain. When he was about 15 or 16, he was captured and enslaved by an Irish chieftain during a raiding party across the sea. He spent several years enslaved in Ireland, herding and tending sheep and swine, and it was during his captivity that Patrick dedicated his life to God. Legend has it that he escaped captivity and Ireland after a dream, in which God instructed him to journey to the Irish coast. Here he found a ship that returned him to his family.

After years of religious study, he became a priest. In a document attributed to him known as The Confession, Patrick heard the voice of the Irish in his dreams, 'crying to thee, come hither and walk with us once more'. Eventually, Pope Clemens commissioned Patrick as bishop to preach the gospel to the Celtic people. Arriving back in Ireland, he travelled across the country, preaching and baptizing, ordaining priests and bishops, erecting churches and establishing places of learning and worship, despite constant threats to his life. It has been said that he and his disciples were responsible for converting almost all the population of Ireland to Christianity.

The most famous legend about St Patrick is that he miraculously drove snakes and all venomous beasts from Ireland by banging a drum. Even to touch Irish soil was seen to be instant death for any such creature. However, this legend is probably a metaphor for his driving the pagans from Ireland, as snakes were often associated with pagan worship.

KEW MUST BE JOKING, JIMI!

Jimi Hendrix was once refused entry to Kew Gardens, because 'we don't let anyone in wearing fancy dress'.

THE TRUTH ABOUT EROS?

The bright lights of Piccadilly Circus are famous throughout the world, and so is the statue of Eros. But look closely and you'll see that Eros isn't actually a statue, but a fountain (on which a small figure rests) commemorating the philanthropic Earl of Shaftesbury. Some say the figure is really a pun on Shaftesbury's name, as the bow doesn't have an arrow in it and is pointing downwards as if the *shaft* has already been shot and is *buried* in the ground.

DEAL LAYABOUTS

Inspiration can come in many forms. In 1703, Daniel Defoe – author of *Robinson Crusoe* – was gobsmacked when he witnessed the unwillingness of the 'men of Deal' to rescue shipwrecked survivors stranded on the Goodwin Sands.

On the night of 26 November 1703, there was a storm which is said to have been the most violent ever in the British Isles. The Channel Squadron, commanded at the time by Rear Admiral Sir Basil Beaumont, was entirely lost. Towards the end the storm, it is said that as many as 1,000 survivors who had washed on to the Goodwins during the night were alive and safe on the sands offshore.

Defoe reported that the assistance of the Deal men was sought, but that they ignored the request because the pickings from the sea were so good at the time. Consequently, everyone that had made it on to the sands perished. After the incident, Defoe wrote a damning ode:

'If I had any satire left to write,
Could I with suited spleen indite,
My verse should blast that fatal town,
And drown'd sailors' widows pull it down;
No footsteps of it should appear,
And ships no more cast anchor there.
The barbarous hated name of Deal shou'd die,
Or be a term of infamy;
And till that's done, the town will stand
A just reproach to all the land.'

A FAIRLY PRIVATE ARMY

The Dukes of Atholl keep Britain's only private army – a unique privilege.

MUSEUMS FOR SPORTS ENTHUSIASTS

Cricket
MCC Museum, Lord's, London
Lancashire County Cricket Club Museum, Old Trafford, Manchester
Warwickshire County Cricket Club Museum, Edgbaston, Birmingham

Football
Arsenal Museum, Highbury, London
Manchester United Museum, Old Trafford, Manchester
Homes of Football, Ambleside, Cumbria
Scottish Football Association Museum, Glasgow
Football Museum, Preston

Golf
Museum of Golf, St Andrews

Horse racing
Cheltenham Racecourse Hall of Fame, Cheltenham
National Horseracing Museum, Newmarket

Motor sports
Brooklands Museum, Weybridge
Donington Collection, Castle Donington

Olympics
Much Wenlock Olympian Society Collection, Much Wenlock

Rowing
River and Rowing Museum, Henley-on-Thames

Rugby
James Gilbert Museum, Rugby
Rugby Football Union Museum, Twickenham
Rugby League Hall of Fame, Huddersfield

Tennis
Royal Tennis Court, Hampton Court Palace
Wimbledon Museum, Wimbledon

MARRIAGE VOWS

I _____, take you _____, to be my wedded wife/husband. To have and to hold, from this day forward, for better, for worse, for richer, for poorer, in sickness or in health, to love and to cherish till death do us part. And hereto I pledge you my faithfulness.

THE HONOURS SYSTEM

Life peerage

All life peers hold the rank of baron and, until the House of Lords Act 1999, used to automatically sit in the House of Lords. These titles exist only during their own lifetime and are not passed to their heirs. Introduced under the Life Peerages Act 1958.

Baronetcy

Similar to knighthood, but an inheritable honour.

Knighthood

Derived from the ideas of medieval chivalry, all knights are allowed to bear the title 'Sir' and gain a number of obscure privileges. Women receiving the honour are styled 'Dame'.

Orders of chivalry

These include the various kinds of knighthoods:

the Most Noble Order of the Garter (1348); initials KG or LG

the Most Ancient and Most Noble Order of the Thistle (1687); initials KT

the Most Honourable Order of the Bath (1725) – has two types, military and civil; ranks are Knight or Dame Grand Cross (GCB), Knight or Dame Commander (KCB or DCB) and Companion (CB)

the Order of Merit (1902) – limited to 24 persons; initials OM

the Most Distinguished Order of St Michael and St George (founded in 1818 by George IV) – ranks are Knight or Dame Grand Cross (GCMG), Knight or Dame Commander (KCMG or DCMG) and Companion (CMG); often given to senior civil servants and said to stand for 'God Calls Me God', 'Kindly Call Me God' and 'Call Me God'

the Royal Victorian Order (1896) – ranks are Knight or Dame Grand Cross (GCVO), Knight or Dame Commander (KCVO or DCVO), Commander (CVO), Lieutenant (LVO) and Member (MVO)

the Royal Victorian Chain (1902)

the Most Excellent Order of the British Empire (1917) – has a military and a civil division; ranks are Knight or Dame Grand Cross (GBE), Knight or Dame Commander (KBE or DBE), Commander (CBE), Officer (OBE) and Member (MBE)

the Order of the Companions of Honour (1917) – limited to 65 people; initials CH

the Most Venerable Order of St John of Jerusalem (1888)

JUBILEE TIME, 2002 STYLE!

Elizabeth II was the oldest monarch to celebrate a Golden Jubilee (aged 76). The youngest was James I (James VI of Scotland), at a sprightly 51 years of age. Before Liz 2, Victoria was the last monarch to celebrate a Golden Jubilee.

In her Jubilee year, the Queen visited 70 cities and towns in England, Scotland, Wales and Northern Ireland, in 50 counties, over 38 days, between May and August.

During the Jubilee, the Queen flew more than 48,000km (30,000 miles) around the UK and the world, including Jamaica, New Zealand and Australia. Her trip to Canada added a further 16,000km (10,000 miles). The 2002 tour was the sixth time in her reign that she has travelled around the world on a single tour.

Perhaps the 'coolest' Jubilee party was in the Antarctic, held by 20 scientists of the British Antarctic Survey, at a temperature of −30°C (−20°F). Celebrations included an outdoor feast and a ration of champagne, plus a game of cricket on the sea ice, along with skiing and sledging.

For the finale of the Jubilee Weekend celebrations, 27 aircraft flew over Buckingham Palace. The fly-past was led by an RAF C17 Globemaster, and ended with Concorde and the Red Arrows trailing red, white and blue.

During the Golden Jubilee Central Weekend, the gardens of Buckingham Palace were used for public concerts for the first time ever.

The Queen is the first member of the royal family to be awarded a gold disc from the recording industry. Within the first week of release, 100,000 copies of the CD of the 'Party at the Palace' were produced by EMI. The concert was one of the most-watched pop events in history, attracting around 200 million viewers from all over the world.

Around 28,000 special coolbags were given free to guests, artists and workers during the two concerts in the gardens of Buckingham Palace. They were packed with goodies including champagne, smoked salmon wrap, 'Jubilee Chicken' and strawberries and cream.

The Queen's Golden Jubilee Award for voluntary service groups was launched during 2002 to honour 'unsung heroes'. It will become an annual award.

The Queen used the following methods of transport during the Jubilee: 777 aeroplane, 727 aeroplane, Falcon aeroplane, 146 aeroplane, helicopter, Skyrail, golden bus, metro, royal train, steam train, aircraft carrier (HMS

Ark Royal), a minesweeper (HMS *Bangor*), royal barge, lifeboat, Gold State Coach, horse-drawn carriage, Rolls Royce, State Land-Rover, Jaguar and new Bentley.

The royal train covered 5,600km (3,500 miles) across England, Scotland and Wales – from Falmouth in Cornwall to Wick in Caithness.

The Golden Jubilee baton travelled through 23 Commonwealth countries, spanning five continents. It spent 50 days on visits in the UK, covering over 8,000km (5,000 miles). There were 5,000 runners in the UK alone.

CONSTITUENCIES WITH THE SMALLEST MAJORITIES SINCE 1945

Winchester 1997 The declared result had Mark Oaten (Liberal Democrat) winning by 2 votes over the Conservative candidate, Gerry Malone. The result was successfully challenged by an election petition, and a by-election resulted in Oaten being returned with a majority of more than 21,000.

Peterborough 1966 Sir Harmar Nicholls (Conservative) beat Michael Ward (Labour) by 3 votes.

Carmarthen February 1974 Gwynoro Jones (Labour) beat Gwynfor Evans (Plaid Cymru), also by 3 votes.

CUMBRIA'S TOP VISITOR ATTRACTIONS (FREE)

Attraction	Location	Visitors in 2002
Carlisle Cathedral	Carlisle	175,456
Lake District Visitor Centre Brockhole	Windermere	165,000
Brougham Hall	Brougham	Around 120,000
Dock Museum	Barrow-in-Furness	Around 100,000
Home of Football	Ambleside	80,000
Cartmel Priory	Cartmel	60,232
Sedbergh National Park Centre	Sedbergh	48,925
Teapottery	Keswick	31,131
Beckstones Art Gallery	Penrith	Around 21,500

THE PARTS OF A BAGPIPE

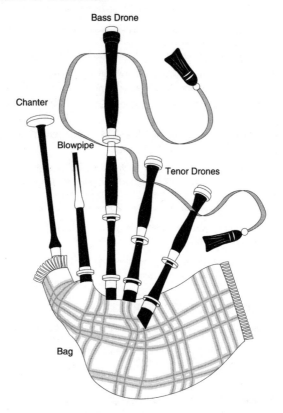

Bass Drone

Chanter

Blowpipe

Tenor Drones

Bag

Chanter The chanter is the reed pipe of the bagpipe, with finger holes on which the melody is played. It contains nine notes, one octave scale and one reed. Other notes and sounds are created when various finger movements or embellishments are used. The novice piper should first use a (less costly) practice chanter to learn the basics of note fingering.

Blowpipe The blowpipe is the part of the bagpipe where air enters and is forced through to fill the bag or pouch. The most popular blowpipe is the 'airstream' blowpipe, which also uses a water trap to prevent water displacement.

Bass drone The bass drone is the longest part of the bagpipe. It comes in two sections, with a reed found at the bottom of the second part. It gives an unvarying sustained base note, which often serves as the tonic in a musical composition. It tunes to a low 'A' note.

Tenor drones The second and third pipes of the bagpipe are similar in size and shape. Each is tuned slightly different from the other, so that a distinct, but similar sound is produced.

Bag The bag is the part of the bagpipe that stores the air used to produce the finished product. One does not actually play the bagpipe by just blowing air right to the chanter and drones; one must first blow the air into the bag, then force the air with one's arm through the chanter and drones. The bag can be made of cowhide or Gore-Tex.

BRAINS AND BACON

Ingredients

430g (1lb) calves' brains

30ml (2tbsp) sherry

100g (4oz) back bacon

5ml (5ml) Worcestershire sauce

25g (1 oz) seasoned flour

300ml (10fl oz) stock

chopped parsley for decoration

Method

1 Soak brains in salted water for 20 minutes.

2 Remove and place in 900ml (1½ pints) boiling water. Reduce heat and simmer for 15 minutes.

3 Drain well and wrap each brain in a slice of bacon. Secure with a wooden cocktail stick and place in a 2½ pint square casserole dish.

4 Make a thickened sauce by mixing seasoned flour with a little stock. Heat gently in a pan adding the rest of the stock, a little at a time. Stir constantly.

5 Lower and cook at 180°C (350°F, gas mark 4) for 20 minutes.

6 Remove from oven and decorate with chopped parsley.

FISH AND CHIPS

Britain's most popular fast food is fish and chips. The dish is very simple: fish (usually cod, haddock or plaice) dipped in a batter made from flour, eggs and water, and then deep-fried in hot fat. Chips are made from thick slices of potato that are deep-fried. Fish and chip shops first made an appearance at the end of the 19th century.

THE MOST EXPENSIVE HOTEL IN BRITAIN

When pop star Michael Jackson was staying at the Lanesborough, like many other mega-rich celebrities, he stayed in the Royal Suite. At £4,500 ($7,470) a night, it claims to be the most expensive hotel accommodation in the UK, and that's before you add on VAT, which takes it to a cool £5,287.50 ($8777.25). Oh, and before you ask, no – dinner and breakfast are *not* included…

WELSH AND ENGLISH WORDS TO 'LAND OF MY FATHERS'

Welsh words
Mae hen wlad fy nhadau yn annwyl i mi,
Gwlad beirdd a chantorion enwogion o fri.
Ei gwrol ryfelwyr, gwlad garwyr tra mad,
Tros ryddid collasant eu gwaed.

CHORUS

Gwlad Gwlad
Pleidiol wyf i'm gwlad;
Tra môr yn fur i'r bur hoff bau,
O bydded i'r hen iaith barhau.

Hen Gymru fynyddig, paradwys y bardd,
Pob dyffryn, pob clogwyn i'm golwg sydd hardd;
Trwy deimlad gwladgarol, mor swynol yw si
Ei nentydd, afonydd, i mi.

CHORUS

Os treisiodd y gelyn fy ngwlad tan ei droed,
Mae hen iaith y Cymry mor fyw ag erioed;
Ni luddiwyd yr awen gan erchyll law brad,
Na thelyn berseiniol fy ngwlad.

CHORUS

English words
The land of my fathers is dear to me,
A land of poets and minstrels, famed men.
Her brave warriors, patriots much blessed,
It was for freedom that they lost their blood.

CHORUS

Homeland! Homeland!
I am devoted to my country;
So long as the sea is a wall to this fair beautiful land,
May the ancient language remain.

Old land of the mountains, the Eden of bards,
Each gorge and each valley a loveliness guards;
Through love of my country, charmed voices will be
Its streams, and its rivers, to me.

CHORUS

Though foemen have trampled my land 'neath their feet,
The language of Cambria still knows no retreat;
The muse is not vanquished by traitor's fell hand,
Nor silenced the harp of my land.

CHORUS

TALES OF 10 DOWNING STREET

10 Downing Street stands on what was once a piece of marshy and boggy land known as Thorney Island or the Island of Thorns. The 12 hectare (30 acre) island lay between two branches of the River Tyburn, which flowed from Hampstead Heath to the Thames.

Until the twentieth century, prime ministers living in Downing Street used to bring their own households with them, including bedding and crockery, as well as furniture. They would move their possessions into the state rooms, and then take them with them when they left office.

Ramsey MacDonald was the first prime minister not to have a personal art collection. He began the convention of borrowing from national collections in order to make the residence into a showcase for traditional and modern British art and craftsmanship.

PLANNED VENUES, SHOULD THE 2012 OLYMPICS BE AWARDED TO LONDON

Lower Lea Valley	cycling, canoeing
Wembley Stadium	football
Olympic Stadium	athletics
Excel Centre, Victoria Dock	fencing, judo, table tennis
Regent's Park	beach volleyball
Stratford	swimming
West Ham	hockey
Hyde Park	triathlon
The Oval	baseball
Trafalgar Square	diving
Millennium Dome	boxing, gymnastics, basketball
Royal Albert Docks	rowing

BOG STANDARDS

Euphemisms for 'toilet' include: bog, cloakroom, close stool, closet, commode, convenience, garderobe, gents', heads, jakes, khazi, ladies', latrine, little boys' room, loo, necessary, netty, place of easement, powder room, privy, smallest room, thunder-box, water-closet and WC.

SOME LOOPY LAWS STILL ON THE STATUTE BOOK

Under the reign of Elizabeth I, any person found guilty of 'harbouring a Catholic priest' would be tortured or even hanged. Any priest of the Catholic faith that was caught would be hanged, drawn and quartered.

With the exception of carrots, most goods may not be sold on Sunday.

All English males over the age 14 are to carry out two or so hours of longbow practice a week, supervised by the local clergy.

London Hackney Carriages (taxis/cabs) must carry a bale of hay and a sack of oats (this was repealed in 1976).

'The severest penalties will be suffered by any commoner who doth permit his animal to have carnal knowledge of a pet of the Royal House' (enacted by George I).

It is illegal to be drunk on licensed premises (in a pub or bar).

It is illegal for two adult men to have sex in the same house as a third person.

Any person found breaking a boiled egg at the sharp end will be sentenced to 24 hours in the village stocks (enacted by Edward VI).

It is illegal to stand within one hundred yards (90m) of the reigning monarch when not wearing socks (enacted by Edward VI).

Chelsea pensioners may not be impersonated.

A bed may not be hung out of a window.

It is illegal for a lady to eat chocolates on a public conveyance.

During his reign, Oliver Cromwell banned the eating of mince pies on Christmas day, as they were insufficiently Puritan.

Any boy under the age of 10 may not see a naked mannequin.

It is illegal to leave baggage unattended.

Picking up abandoned baggage is an act of terrorism.

In Chester, one can only shoot a Welsh person with a bow and arrow inside the city walls and after midnight.

In Hereford, one may not shoot a Welsh person on Sunday with a longbow in the Cathedral Close.

In York, excluding Sundays, it is perfectly legal to shoot a Scotsman with a bow and arrow.

Since 1313, it is illegal for an MP to enter the House of Commons wearing a full suit of armour.

A licence is required to keep a lunatic.

CULLODEN

The Battle of Culloden – the last true battle fought on British soil – took place in 1746, between the forces of Bonnie Prince Charlie's Jacobite rebels and the British troops of the Duke of Cumberland. It was the decisive conflict in Scotland's attempt to gain independence. Around 5,000 Scots lined up against 9,000 English and it proved to be an almighty anticlimax, for the battle was over within 40 minutes, during which time the English slaughtered more than 1,000 Scots, with the loss of just 250 of their own troops.

FLOWER POWER

England

Ireland

Scotland

Wales

The national flower of England is the rose, and has been adopted as England's emblem since the time of the Wars of the Roses – civil wars (1455–85) between the royal houses of Lancaster (whose emblem was a red rose) and York (the white rose). Future king Henry VII defeated King Richard III at Bosworth on 22 August 1485, and united the two roses into the Tudor rose (a red rose with a white centre) when he married Elizabeth of York. The national flower of Northern Ireland is the shamrock, a three-leafed plant similar to clover. It is said to have been used by St Patrick to illustrate the doctrine of the Holy Trinity. The Scottish national flower is the thistle, a prickly leafed purple flower that was first used in the 15th century as a symbol of defence. The three flowers – the rose, thistle and shamrock – are often displayed beneath the shield of the Royal Coat of Arms. The national flower of Wales is usually considered to be the daffodil, which is traditionally worn on St David's Day. However, the leek is also considered to be a traditional Welsh emblem, possibly because its colours (white over green) echo the ancient Welsh standard.

BRITAIN'S GROTTIEST PLACES ACCORDING TO 'CRAP MAP'

Hull
Cumbernauld
Morecambe
Hythe
Winchester
Liverpool
St Andrews
Bexhill-on-Sea
Basingstoke
Hackney
Portsmouth
Stockport
Crouch End
St John's Wood
Croydon
Islington
Peterborough
Wolverhampton
Didcot
Ascot
Brighton
Aldeburgh
Leiston
Ipswich
Hayling Island
Horsham
Mirfield
Tintern
Peterhead
Oxford

LLANFAIR...ETC

The longest place name in Britain is 58 letters long and belongs to the Anglesey village known as
Llanfairpwllgwyngyllgogerychwyrndrobwllllantysiliogogogoch,
which translates as 'The church of St Mary in a hollow of white hazel near a rapid whirlpool and near St Tysilio's church by the red cave'. The name was invented in the 19th century in order to lure gullible tourists to what is an otherwise unremarkable Welsh village.

TROOPING THE COLOUR

The custom of trooping the colour dates back to the 17th century, during Charles II's reign. A regiment's colours were used as a rallying point in battle and were therefore trooped in front of the soldiers every day to make sure that each man could recognise those of his own regiment. In London, the Foot Guards used to do this from 1755, as part of their daily Guard Mounting on Horse Guards, and the ceremonial of the present parade runs along similar lines.

The parade was first carried out to celebrate the sovereign's birthday in 1805, and is now held on the occasion of the Queen's Official Birthday in June, carried out by her personal troops (the Household Division) on Horse Guard's Parade, with the Queen herself attending and taking the salute. Since 1987, the Queen has attended in a carriage rather than riding (which she did on 36 occasions, riding sidesaddle and wearing the uniform of the regiment whose colour was being trooped). The regiments take their turn for this honour, in strict rotation.

Over 1,400 officers and men are on parade, together with 200 horses, and more than 400 musicians from 10 bands and corps of drums march and play as one. The parade route extends from Buckingham Palace along The Mall to Horse Guard's Parade, Whitehall and back again. The Officer in Command of the parade gives 113 words of command. As the clock on the Horse Guard's Building strikes 11 o'clock, the Royal Procession arrives and the Queen takes the Royal Salute. The parade begins with the inspection – the Queen driving slowly down the ranks of all eight Guards and then past the Household Cavalry. After the event, the royal family gathers on the balcony of Buckingham Palace to watch an RAF fly-past.

THE TYBURN TREE

On the traffic island at the junction of Edgware Road and Marble Arch, there is a plaque (which most people ignore) marking the site of the Tyburn Tree, London's main execution spot, where about 50,000 people were executed. Nearby, in Bayswater Road, is the Shrine and Tyburn Convent, where the nuns still pray for the souls of those whose lost their lives.

BLINK AND YOU'LL MISS IT

Consisting of just 2,000 people, St David's in south Wales is dominated by its own cathedral, which by law makes it a city – the smallest in Britain.

THE NORTHWEST'S TOP VISITOR ATTRACTIONS (PAID)

Attraction	Location	Visitors in 2002
Chester Zoo	Chester	1,134,949
Mersey Ferries	Wallasey	Around 690,000
Tatton Park	Knutsford	Around 564,300
Knowsley Safari Park	Prescot	447,200
Blackpool Zoo Park	Blackpool	Around 285,000
Manchester United Museum	Old Trafford	219,551
Lancaster Leisure Park	Lancaster	Around 215,000

THE REAL ST DAVID

David is thought to have been born to the royal house of Ceredigion in around AD 530, although another theory has his birthplace at Henvynyw (Vetus-Menevia) in Cardiganshire. He became a monk and founded the monastery of Mynyw (Menevia) at what is now St David's in Pembrokeshire. (The current St David's Cathedral was built on the traditional location of David's monastery.) Like many contemporary church leaders, he was a bishop as well as an abbot, and his monastery was a popular centre of learning, especially among Irish scholars.

It seems likely that David died around 589, a respected and influential leader of the early Christian church in Wales. It is also probable that, under David and his fellows, the Welsh undertook a certain amount of missionary work, though little of this was aimed at the neighbouring pagan English – rather their fellow Celts in Cornwall, Ireland and Brittany.

A host of legends sprang up about David after he died. One tale tells how the Welsh were preparing to do battle with the Saxons and, on the advice of David, they all put leeks in their hats so they could easily distinguish themselves from their enemies in the heat of battle.

LEFT–RIGHT–LEFT AT THE SAVOY

The Savoy Hotel stands on the site of the Palace of the Savoy – have a look at the panels on each side of the hotel's approach that record its history. Cars coming from the Strand to the Savoy must travel on the right-hand side of the road, not the left – the only place in Britain where this happens.

THE MADNESS OF UK LOTTERY WINNERS

Some of the most unusual purchases made by National Lottery winners include breast enlargements, a racehorse and a castle.

Just by chance, a winner's girlfriend checked his trouser pockets before she put his jeans into the washing machine and found a jackpot winning ticket worth around £1.5 million ($2.5 million). Lucky…

A winner was dancing in the street outside his house, jumping up and down with excitement and broke his leg!

The longest winners' celebration was by a London pub syndicate. They celebrated for almost two weeks!

Neighbours called the police because they thought the people living next door were being burgled, due to the amount of noise. They were in fact celebrating their jackpot win of £2 million ($3.3 million).

Judith Knox from Morpeth hid her ticket in her bra after discovering that she and her partner had won £102,262 ($170,000). Other unusual places where lottery winners choose to hide their tickets include socks, shoes, freezers and biscuit tins. An elderly gentleman put his ticket in his underpants on Saturday night and did not remove it until Monday morning, while another man taped his ticket to his chest.

When syndicate leader Peter Cockhrane realised his numbers had come up, his main concern was preventing his 5-year-old daughter Rachel from defacing the winning ticket – worth £101,288 ($168,150). So he hid the ticket in one of the drawers under his bed.

Phillip and Shirley Hunter won £1.3 million ($2.2 million) after selecting numbers from balls in Hilda – their tumble dryer.

GIANT IRON

On the slopes of a mountain named Yr Eifl in the Llyn Peninsula in North Wales is the largest Iron Age fort in northwest Europe – Tre'r Ceiri (meaning 'Town of Giants'). At a height of 400m (1310ft) above sea level, the settlement includes the remains of 150 stone huts constructed some time around 200 BC, but still occupied at the time of the Roman invasions of Britain around 300 years later. The stone wall surrounding the fort is still as high as 4m (13ft) in parts.

TOP TOWNS VISITED BY TOURISTS EACH MONTH

London 11,600,000

Edinburgh 850,000

Birmingham 670,000

Manchester 590,000

Glasgow 400,000

Oxford 390,000

Bristol 310,000

Cambridge 280,000

Cardiff 280,000

Newcastle-upon-Tyne 240,000

Brighton and Hove 230,000

York 230,000

Bath 200,000

Nottingham 200,000

Liverpool 190,000

Inverness 180,000

Coventry 160,000

Reading 150,000

Canterbury 150,000

Leeds 140,000

BRITAIN'S BEST-PAID POSTCODES (PER ANNUM)

Purley, Surrey, CR8 3	£53,900 ($89,500)
Effingham, Surrey, KT24 5	£52,700 ($87,500)
Hampstead, North London, NW3 7	£51,000 ($84,600)
Chandler's Cross, Herts, WD3 4	£50,700 ($84,200)
Radlett, Herts, WD7 7	£50,300 ($83,500)
Wokingham, Berks, RG40 5	£49,700 ($82,500)
Gerrards Cross, Bucks, SL9 8	£49,400 ($82,000)
Gerrards Cross, Bucks, SL9 7	£49,400 ($82,000)
Bayswater, London, W8 7	£49,300 ($81,800)
Kensington Gardens, London, W8 5	£49,200 ($81,700)

MAIL-ORDER MAN

Sometime in 1859, astute businessman Pryce Pryce-Jones, of Newtown, Montgomeryshire, began to cater to the needs of many of his rural customers by offering goods for sale through the mail. Many of the area's farmers lived in isolated valleys or in mountain terrain, and had little time or suitable transportation to come into town for their many needs. The Pryce-Jones Mail Order business was the perfect answer, especially since the Post Office reforms of the 1840s had made the mail service cheap and reliable. The Newtown Warehouses, packed with goods, began a service that quickly caught on in the United States, with its even greater distances and scattered population. As we know only too well from our mailboxes that seem to be forever bulging with catalogues, mail-order shopping was here to stay.

SNOWDON'S RAILWAY

The Snowdonia Mountain Railway was built in 1896, and is unique because it is Britain's only rack and pinion railway. (Each locomotive has a cog wheel that grips a toothed rail on the track to stop the train sliding down the mountain.) It has a rare 2ft 7in (79cm) gauge and runs from the town of Llanberis up the side of Wales' highest mountain to within a few feet of its 1,085m (3,560ft) summit – a journey of 8km (5 miles) that takes an hour to complete.

HOW TO MAKE A MARTINI LIKE JAMES BOND

Bond looked carefully at the barman.
'A dry martini,' he said. 'One. In a deep champagne goblet.'
'Oui, monsieur.'
'Just a moment. Three measures of Gordon's, one of vodka, half a measure of Kina Lillet. Shake it very well until it's ice-cold, then add a large thin slice of lemon-peel. Got it?'
'Certainly, monsieur.' The barman seemed pleased with the idea.

From *Casino Royale* by Ian Fleming

TEA SIPPERS

The British are renowned for their love of tea, but the world's biggest tea drinkers are the Irish, who drink 1,184 cups per person each year. The British drink just 1,025, making them the fifth biggest consumers behind the Turks (1,056), the Kuwaitis (1,069) and the Libyans (1,074).

LANGUAGES ON THE WORLD SERVICE...

Arabic, Albanian, Azeri, Bengali, Bulgarian, Burmese, Caribbean English, Chinese, Croatian, Czech, French, Greek, Hausa, Hindi, Hungarian, Indonesian, Kazakh, Kinyarwanda, Kirundi, Kyrgyz, Macedonian, Nepali, Pashto, Persian, Polish, Portuguese, African Portuguese, Romanian, Russian, Serbian, Sinhala, Slovene, Slovak, Somali, Spanish, Swahili, Tamil, Thai, Turkish, Ukrainian, Urdu, Uzbek and Vietnamese.

WAS IST DAS?

King George I of England could not speak English. He was born and raised in Germany, and never learned to speak English, even though he was king from 1714 to 1727. He left the running of the country to his ministers, thereby creating the first government cabinet.

BRITAIN'S POETS LAUREATE

*1617	Ben Jonson
*1638	Sir William Davenant
1668	John Dryden
1689	Thomas Shadwell
1692	Nahum Tate
1715	Nicholas Rowe
1718	Laurence Eusden
1730	Colley Cibber
1757	William Whitehead
1785	Thomas Wharton
1790	Henry James Pye
1813	Robert Southey
1843	William Wordsworth
1850	Alfred, Lord Tennyson
1896	Alfred Austin
1913	Robert Bridges
1930	John Masefield
1968	Cecil Day-Lewis
1972	Sir John Betjeman
1984	Ted Hughes
1999	Andrew Motion

*The post of was not officially recognised until 1668.

SOME OF BRITAIN'S COLD WAR NUCLEAR BUNKERS

Kelvedon Hatch, Essex

Built in 1952 and completed in August 1953 by the Air Ministry, this bunker began its life as the Fighter Command Metropolitan Sector Operations Centre under the ROTOR system. This continued until the 1960s, when ROTOR became obsolete and the life of the bunker changed. For a short while, it was under Civil Defence and UKWMO (United Kingdom Warning and Monitoring Organisation) then in the late 1960s it was converted into a Regional Government Headquarters. It stayed that way until 1994, when the bunker was decommissioned.

Mistley, Essex

Meant for Essex County Council, Mistley has been restored extremely well and has nearly all its original equipment. It is a semi-sunk bunker, with one floor above ground and one floor below.

Anstruther, Fife, near St Andrews

The site first started life as an RAF radar station in early World War II, and over the years it was equipped with different types of radar units, all of which have long since been removed. It became the Scottish Northern Zone Headquarters in 1973. Anstruther opened to the public as a museum in 1994.

Reading, Berks

Situated in the main Reading University campus at Whiteknights, it was built in 1953 along with 12 other identical bunkers (at Newcastle, Leeds, Nottingham, Cambridge, London, Bristol, Cardiff, Birmingham, Manchester, Edinburgh, Tunbridge Wells and Belfast).

Southampton

The bunker is now in the back garden of a private house in Somerset Avenue in Southampton. It is not visible from the road and the owner does not welcome casual visitors.

GANGSTERS IN THE HOOD

Bethnal Green has been the legendary haunt of many an East End gangster, but none as notorious as Ronnie and Reggie Kray, who ran their empire from an unremarkable flat at 178 Vallance Road. After years flouting the law, they were eventually jailed in 1969 after being convicted of the murder of Jack 'The Hat' McVitie in the Blind Beggar pub on Whitechapel Road.

THE NORTHWEST'S TOP VISITOR ATTRACTIONS (FREE)

Attraction	Location	Visitors in 2002
Blackpool Pleasure Beach	Blackpool	6,200,000
Pleasureland Theme Park	Southport	Around 2,000,000
Chester Cathedral	Chester	Around 850,000
The Lowry	Salford	Around 810,200
Tate Liverpool	Liverpool	504,062
Science and Industry in Manchester	Manchester	Around 445,273
Liverpool Anglican Cathedral	Liverpool	342,261
Blakemere Craft Centre	Northwich	Around 335,000
Liverpool Museum	Liverpool	Around 303,621
Imperial War Museum North	Manchester	290,467

POTEEN, ANYONE?

Legend has it that poteen (pronounced 'puh-cheen') or *poitín*, meaning 'little pot' (highlighting the small-scale home production), has been produced in Ireland since the time when potatoes were first harvested. Also known as Irish Moonshine Whiskey or Mountain Dew, its taste has been described as distinctive and unique, with dry, grainy kicks. Its aftertaste can have hints of toffee and other flavours, and tends to sweeten as it develops.

In 1661, the English, attempting to rebuild their postwar treasury, decided to introduce a charge on spirits. In Ireland, this forbade private distillation that was not licensed by the State, so to distil poteen was against the law and led to a substantial section of the nation being deemed criminals.

The actual recipe for poteen is a closely guarded secret, though it is said that a good poteen should only contain the finest malt yeast, barley, sugar and water. A beer (or baor) was achieved by fermenting the ingredients in wooden barrels, for around three weeks. This was then distilled, usually in a home-made still, to produce a clear spirit with a distinct smell.

BRITAIN'S TOP VISITOR ATTRACTIONS (FREE)

Name	Location	Visitors in 2002
Blackpool Pleasure Beach	Blackpool	6,200,000
Tate Modern	London	4,618,632
British Museum	London	4,607,311
National Gallery	London	Around 4,130,973
Natural History Museum	London	2,957,501
Victoria and Albert Museum	London	2,661,338
Science Museum	London	2,628,374
Pleasureland Theme Park	Southport	Around 2,000,000
Eastbourne Pier	Eastbourne	Around 1,900,000
York Minster	York	Around 1,570,500
Pleasure Beach	Great Yarmouth	Around 1,500,000
National Portrait Gallery	London	1,484,331
Tate Britain	London	1,178,235
Kelvingrove Art Gallery	Glasgow	Around 955,671
Somerset House	London	Around 900,000
Flamingo Family Fun Park	Hastings	900,000
Chester Cathedral	Chester	Around 850,000
The Lowry	Salford	Around 810,200
Poole Pottery	Poole	808,725

FACTS ABOUT THE ROBIN, BRITAIN'S FAVOURITE BIRD

Habitat	Woodlands, gardens, parks, forest edge
Nest	Holes in trees, wall recesses, dense climbers, open-fronted nesting boxes and unusual items such as kettles and gardening jacket pockets
Eggs	2 broods of 5 or 6 eggs, blue and speckled with red
Food	Insects, worms, fruit, mealworms, waxworms, peanuts, seeds, seed mixes, fat bars, grated cheese, pinhead oatmeal
Voice	Call is a short hard 'tick'; song is a well-known pleasant warbling

BRITAIN'S FAVOURITE MEAL

Chicken tikka masala (CTM), voted Britain's favourite meal, has a truly post-colonial history and was produced when one of the world's greatest cuisines found itself confronted by a British palate unused to anything spicier than table salt. Legend has it that one obstinate diner demanded gravy on tandoori chicken. A bemused chef responded by adding a tin of Campbell's tomato soup and a pinch of spices.

Sainsbury's sell 1.6 million CTM meals every year and stock 16 CTM-related products, including CTM pasta sauce. Other derivations include CTM crisps, CTM pizzas, CTM kievs and Marks and Spencer's famous CTM sandwiches (18 tonnes/20 tons devoured every week).

A survey of 48 different CTMs, carried out by the Real Curry Restaurant Guide in 1998, found that the only common ingredient was chicken.

23 million portions a year are sold in Indian restaurants.

10 tonnes (11 tons) of CTM a day are produced by Noon Products, destined for supermarkets.

Most schools and charities in Sylhet, Bangladesh, are run by proceeds from the sale of CTM.

Chef Iftekar Haris from Newport, Gwent, has written a musical in praise of it.

Organisers of Kingfisher National Curry Day claim that if all the portions sold in one year in the UK were stacked, they would constitute a tikka tower 2,770 times taller than the Greenwich Millennium Dome.

THE WOBBLY BRIDGE

The £18.2 million ($30 million) Millennium Bridge is central London's first new river crossing for more than a century, though it had to be shut three days after it opened in the summer of 2000. It is thought that around 180,000 people crossed the bridge in its first weekend, which caused it to wobble from side to side.

A series of 90 dampers (shock absorbers) had to be fitted to the 350m (1,148ft) suspension bridge, which links the City of London and the South Bank of the Thames. Architects, engineers and workers from surrounding offices were marshalled en masse across the bridge to check on the success of the £5 million ($8.3 million) repairs. Luckily, they were successful.

MAP OF COUNTIES

MOST COMMON MURDER METHODS IN THE UK

1. Sharp instrument
2. Strangulation and asphyxiation
3. Hitting and kicking
4. Unidentified means
5. Blunt instrument

6. Shooting
7. Poison or drugs
8. Motor vehicle
9. Burning
10. Drowning

FACTS ABOUT THE BRITISH BANGER

Approximately 250,000 tonnes (275,000 tons) of sausage are consumed each year – that's around 4.5kg (10lb) per person.

Hot-dog sellers do more business outside strip clubs than any tourist landmark in London.

In AD 320, Emperor Constantine banned sausage eating as 'sinful' because of their links to pagan festivals.

In 1958, sausages appeared on more than 200 seaside postcards.

British university students have voted a sausage as student union president on no fewer than six occasions.

A dog who could say 'sausages' became a star after appearing on Esther Rantzen's *That's Life* TV show in the 1970s.

Chasing the Sausage was a popular Elizabethan pub game. It involved the man hiding a sausage down his pantaloons, which then had to be found by a blindfolded wench.

The highest accolade for any sausage maker is the *Meat Trades Journal* Champion of Champions.

Ready-cooked sausages are the top-selling party food for office Christmas parties.

Sausages got the nickname 'banger' during World War II, because wartime sausages contained so much water they tended to explode when fried.

The world's longest sausage was made in October 2000 during British Sausage Appreciation Week. It weighed 15.5 tonnes (17 tons) and was 56km (35 miles) long.

The meat for Wall's famous sausages was originally ground by a donkey working on a treadmill in a cellar at 113 Jermyn Street, London.

The most expensive sausages in Britain are made from fillet steak and champagne, and cost £20 ($33) a pack.

British households spend more than £450 million ($750 million) on sausages every year.

There are over 470 recipes and flavours for sausages in Britain.

BRITAIN'S RICHEST TOP 10

Hans Rausing (food packaging) – £3.4 billion ($5.6 billion)
The British-based Swedish industrialist is the son of Ruben Rausing, inventor of the cardboard milk carton.

Lord Sainsbury and family (retailing) – £3.1 billion ($5.1 billion)
In 1998, Lord Sainsbury quit the family supermarket company (J Sainsbury) after 35 years, and has joined the Government as Science Minister.

George Soros (finance) – £2 billion ($3.3 billion)
The Hungarian-born financier was made famous for his role in knocking Britain out of the European exchange-rate mechanism in 1992.

Joseph Lewis (finance) – £1.75 billion ($2.9 billion)
The fortune of the London-born financier, who lives in the Bahamas, includes proceeds from foreign exchange dealing and an art collection.

Duke of Westminster (land and property) – £1.75 billion ($2.9 billion)
The Duke's Grosvenor estates property empire includes the 300 'golden acres' of London's Mayfair.

Lady Grantchester and the Moores family (stores, mail order and football pools) – £1.5 billion ($2.5 billion)
Lady Grantchester leads the family that owns the Littlewoods empire.

Garfield Weston and family (food) – £1.5 billion ($2.5 billion)
Mr Weston is chairman and chief executive of Associated British Foods, which he has turned from a troubled food group into a multinational business producing staples such as bread and sugar.

Sri and Gopi Hinduja (trading and finance) – £1.3 billion ($2.2 billion)
The brothers control a global business empire, Hinduja Group, started by their late father, a Bombay trader. In 1998 they agreed to underwrite the Millennium Dome's troubled £6m spirit zone.

Bruno Schroder and family (banking) – £1.3 billion ($2.2 billion)
Schroder's is Britain's last independent quoted investment bank of any size. The Schroder family, led by Bruno Schroder, holds 48% of the shares.

Richard Branson (travel, retailing and entertainment) – £1.2 billion ($2 billion)
The well-known head of the Virgin empire, the flagship of which is the Virgin Atlantic airline.

Lakshmi Mittal (steel) – £1.2 billion ($2 billion)
Mr Mittal is the son of an Indian steel magnate. He built his Ispat
International steel group (which floated in New York in 1997) by acquiring
unwanted assets and turning them round through investment and cost-cutting.

BEATLES MANIA

Abbey Road – an otherwise unremarkable street in St John's Wood, north
London – has assumed legendary status thanks to Abbey Road Studios,
where The Beatles recorded almost their entire body of work. After the
band were pictured crossing it on the cover of their *Abbey Road* album, the
pedestrian crossing outside the studio has become a shrine. The fact that
Paul McCartney is barefoot on the photo was (for some reason) taken as
evidence by conspiracy theorists that he was, in fact, dead.

NORTHUMBERLAND'S TOP VISITOR ATTRACTIONS (PAID)

Attraction	Location	Visitors in 2002
New Metroland	Gateshead	Around 810,000
The North of England Open Air Museum	Beamish	311,692
The Alnwick Garden	Alnwick	304,602
Alnwick Castle	Alnwick	139,428
Cragside House and Gardens	Rothbury	138,236
Wallington House Walled Garden	Cambo	1,29,028
Bamburgh Castle	Bamburgh	109,569
Housesteads Roman Fort	Hexham	108,975
Saltburn's Inclined Tramway	Saltburn-by-the-Sea	101,720
White House Farm Centre	North White	Around 100,000

WHAT'S THE STORY, BERWICK STREET?

Renowned for its collection of record shops, Berwick Street (in Soho,
London) was used by Manchester band Oasis for the cover of their second
album, *(What's The Story?) Morning Glory.*

SOME UNEXPECTED PLACES WHERE HIGHLAND GAMES ARE HELD

Angels Camp, California

Bridgeport, West Virginia

Cape Breton Island, Nova Scotia

Carrollton, Kentucky

Gatlinburg, Tennessee

Grand Prairie, Alberta

Jacksonville, Florida

Las Vegas, Nevada

Los Gatos, California

Pelham, Alabama

Pembroke Pines, Florida

Prince Frederick, Maryland

St Catherine's, Ontario

St Paul, Minnesota

San Antonio, Texas

Sarasota, Florida

Scottsdale, Arizona

Waikiki, Hawaii

Winter Springs, Florida

Woodland Park, Colorado

GREYFRIARS BOBBY

John 'Jock' Gray was an Edinburgh policeman during the 1850s, and his companion and police watchdog was a Skye terrier named Bobby. Gray died of tuberculosis in 1858 and was buried in Greyfriars Kirk graveyard. Bobby followed the funeral procession, and was taken home afterwards, but the little dog soon escaped and took up residence on his master's grave. Various people took pity on the forlorn little fellow. James Brown, the church gardener, provided Bobby with food and water even though his duties included keeping dogs and children out of the graveyard, and James Anderson (who lived nearby) would try to coax Bobby into his house during inclement weather, but the dog would howl so pitifully to be let out that eventually a shelter was built for him near the grave.

Bobby remained at Gray's grave for the rest of his life – a total of 14 years. However, because he was a stray, there was some question as to whether he should be allowed to wander the streets of Edinburgh without a licence. If nobody had been willing to pay, then the penalty for Bobby would have been death, but the Lord Provost of Edinburgh, Sir William Chambers, came to the rescue. He was so impressed by Bobby's devotion that he agreed to purchase the licence – and did so for every year thereafter.

Bobby's expression of devotion quickly made him a local celebrity in Edinburgh. His statue now stands on Princes Street near Waverley Station. His collar (inscribed with the words 'Greyfriars Bobby from the Lord Provost, 1867, licensed') and dinner bowl are on display in the Huntly House Museum on the Royal Mile, and his grave always displays fresh flowers.

AN ANNOYING RELIC

The Ballylumford Dolmen, on Islandmagee near Larne, County Antrim, is a spectacular Neolithic monument, but is also Ireland's most problematic. It is situated in the small front garden of an occupied house, stops daylight from entering the front of the house and forces the occupants to gain access through a side door.

NORTHUMBERLAND'S TOP VISITOR ATTRACTIONS (FREE)

Attraction	Location	Visitors in 2002
Baltic: The Centre for Contemporary Art	Gateshead	587,026
Sunderland Museum and Winter Gardens	Sunderland	352,306
Barter Books	Alnwick	Around 250,000
St Aidan's Winery	Holy Island	Around 225,000
Carlisle Park	Morpeth	Around 190,000
Northumbria Craft Centre and Chantry Bagpipe Museum	Morpeth	157,243
South Shields Museum and Art Gallery	South Shields	148,350
Causey Arch and Picnic Area	Stanley	125,605
Durham Dales Centre	Stanhope	112,494

AN A–Z OF OBSCURE DIALLING CODES

Achnashellach **01520**

Barnham Broom **01603**

Childs Ercall **01952**

Derrygonnelly **028 686**

Edzell **01356**

Forgue **01466**

Gwynfe **01550**

Hazelbury Bryan **01258**

Ibstock **01530**

Joppa **01292**

Knockin **01691**

Layer-de-la-Haye **01206**

Meigle **01828**

Nebo **01974**

Old Dailly **01465**

Pluckley **01233**

Quatt **01746**

Rhosllanerchrugog **01978**

Scarp **01859**

Teffont **01722**

Uig **01470**

Voe **01806**

Wem **01939**

Yatton **01934**

Zelah **01872**

TV SCHEDULE FOR THE FIRST NIGHT OF ITV, 22 SEPTEMBER 1959

7:15 The Ceremony At Guildhall
The Guests Arrive

7:30 The Hallé Orchestra
'Cockaigne (In London Town)' by Sir Edward Elgar
The National Anthem

7:45 Inaugural Speeches
The Lord Mayor of London, Sir Seymour Howard
The Postmaster-General, Charles Hill
Chairman of the ITA, Sir Kenneth Clark

8:00 Channel 9
A sparkling Variety show from ABC's Television Theatre. Appearing tonight, introduced by Jack Jackson, are: Shirley Abicair, Elizabeth Allen, Daphene Batchelor, Billy Cotton, Reg Dixon, Lucille Graham, Hughie Green, John Hanson, Sheila Mathe   ws, Michael Miles, Bessie Rofers, Shirley Norman, Leslie Randall, Derek Roy, Joy Shelton, Harry Secombe, Leslie Welch, Kip Van Nash, Theda Sisters and the George Carden Dancers

8:40 Drama: Robert Morley introduces
The Importance Of Being Earnest (excerpt)
Starring Dame Edith Evans, Margaret Leighton and Sir John Gielgud
Baker's Dozen
Starring Pamela Brown, Alec Guinness and Faith Brook
Private Lives
Staring Kay Hammond and John Clements

9:10 Professional Boxing
Terrence Murphy v Lew Lazar
12-round contest for the Southern Area Middleweight Championship

10:00 News and Newsreel

10:15 Gala Night At The Mayfair
Leslie Mitchell introduces some of the guests

10:30 Star Cabaret
With Music by Billy Ternant and his Orchestra

10:50 Preview
A glimpse of some of the programmes to come on Independent Television during the coming months

11:00 Epilogue
The National Anthem and close-down

SOME FAMOUS LAST WORDS

Lady Nancy Astor
'Am I dying or is is this my birthday?'

Thomas A Becket
'For the name of Jesus and the protection of the church I am ready to embrace death.'

Robert the Bruce
'Now, God be with you, my dear children. I have breakfasted with you and shall sup with my Lord Jesus Christ.'

Charlie Chaplin
Priest: 'May God have mercy on your soul'
Chaplin: 'Why not? After all, it belongs to him.'

Charles II
'I have been a most unconscionable time dying, but I beg you to excuse it. Let not poor Nelly [his mistress, Nell Gwynn] starve.'

Henry VIII
'All is lost. Monks, monks, monks!'

Anne Boleyn
'The executioner is, I believe, very expert, and my neck is very slender.'

Oliver Cromwell
'My design is to make what haste I can to be gone.'

Charles Darwin
'I am not the least afraid to die.'

Elizabeth I
'All my possessions for a moment of time.'

Lord Byron
'Now I shall go to sleep. Good night.'

James, Duke of Monmouth
'Do not hack me as you did my Lord Russell.'

Captain Lawrence Oates
'I am just going outside and may be some time.'

William Pitt
'Oh, my country! How I leave my country!'

George Sanders
'Dear World. I am leaving you because I am bored. I feel I have lived long enough. I am leaving you with your worries in this sweet cesspool. Good luck.'

HG Wells
'Go away. I'm all right.'

William IV
To his page, Sir Walthen Waller:
'Wally, what is this? It is death, my boy: they have deceived me.'

George V
'Bugger Bognor.'

NO-WIN-STANLEY

Henry Winstanley was an artist and engraver, who, among other things, designed playing cards.

On 14 July 1696, he began building the first Eddystone Lighthouse. The first summer he made 12 holes in the rock and fastened 12 great irons to hold the work that was to be done afterwards. In the second year, he erected a round pillar 3.7m (12ft) high and 4.3m (14ft) in diameter on the Rock, and in the third year, the remainder of the wooden lighthouse was carried up to a height of 24m (80ft), and a weathervane placed on top. At last it was finished, and on the night of 14 November 1698, the lighthouse was lit up with tallow candles.

'I only wish that I may be in the lighthouse in circumstances that will test its strength to the utmost,' Winstanley said. Unfortunately, he was to get his wish. On the afternoon of 26 November 1703, he set off in dirty weather from Plymouth for the Eddystone Rock, deciding to stay there for the night. Then came the Great Storm, with its dramatic consequences.

We know no more of what happened, except that when daylight dawned on the morning of 27 November, and men looked out towards the Eddystone Rock, there were no signs of a lighthouse. The Rock was as bare as it used to be. Winstanley's structure, along with its designer, had been swept away for ever by the Great Storm.

SALFORD BY THE SEA?

Although it is 56km (35 miles) from the sea, Salford Docks – now renamed Salford Quays – was Britain's third-busiest port in its prime, thanks to the Manchester Ship Canal, which connected the city to Liverpool.

CHURCHILL'S 'FIGHT ON THE BEACHES' SPEECH, 4 JUNE 1940

'The British Empire and the French Republic, linked together in their cause and in their need, will defend to the death their native soil, aiding each other like good comrades to the utmost of their strength. Even though large tracts of Europe and many old and famous States have fallen or may fall into the grip of the Gestapo and all the odious apparatus of Nazi rule, we shall not flag or fail. We shall go on to the end, we shall fight in France, we shall fight on the seas and oceans, we shall fight with growing confidence and growing strength in the air, we shall defend our Island, whatever the cost may be, we shall fight on the beaches, we shall fight on the landing grounds, we shall fight in the fields and in the streets, we shall fight in the hills; we shall never surrender, and even if, which I do not for a moment believe, this Island or a large part of it were subjugated and starving, then our Empire beyond the seas, armed and guarded by the British Fleet, would carry on the struggle, until, in God's good time, the New World, with all its power and might, steps forth to the rescue and the liberation of the old.'

EATING OUT?

There is no excuse to go hungry or thirsty in London. The capital has more than 6,000 restaurants 3,500 pubs and 1,200 hotels (of which 300 have full restaurant facilities). In fact, 16 per cent of the UK's restaurants are located in London. The city boasts 31 Michelin-starred restaurants, which is more than any other city outside Paris. There is only 1 three-starred restaurant – Gordon Ramsay. There are 4 two-starred restaurants and 25 one-starred restaurants.

BALTIC: THE CENTRE FOR CONTEMPORARY ART

Hailed as an 'Art Factory', the Baltic Centre for Contemporary Art provides an imposing and ambitious sight on the south bank of the River Tyne. The £46 million ($76 million) transformation of the disused Baltic Flour Mill into a contemporary art venue has provided Gateshead with one of the largest art spaces in Europe. The 42m- (138ft-) high silo is all that remains of the sprawling mill since its doors closed for the last time in 1982, and it has drawn predictable comparisons with the Tate Modern, which is housed in a disused power station on the banks of the Thames. Architect Dominic Wilson triumphed in an international competition with his innovative design to transform the warehouse. He was awarded the contract in 1994 and said he had always been mindful of the landmark status the Baltic held on Tyneside.

MILITARY MOTTOS

'Serve To Lead'
Royal Military Academy Sandhurst

'Who Dares Wins'
Special Air Service (SAS) Regiment

'Not By Strength But By Guile'
British Special Boat Service (SBS)

Utrinque Paratus
('Ready For Anything')
Parachute Regiment

Ubique Quo Fas et Gloria Ducunt
('Everywhere where right and glory lead us')
Royal Regiment of Artillery

'Fear Naught'
Royal Tank Regiment

Celer et Audax
('Swift and Bold')
Royal Greenjackets

Per Mare, Per Terram
('By Land, By Sea')
Royal Marines

Per Ardua Ad Astra
('Through Adversity to the Stars')
Royal Air Force

Per Ardua
('Through Adversity')
Royal Air Force Regiment

Nemo me impune lacessit
('None attack me with impunity')
Scots Guards, Royal Scots, Cameroonians, Black Watch, 42nd Highlanders

'Death or Glory'
Queen's Royal Lancers

Nec aspera terrent
('Difficulties be damned')
The Prince of Wales' own Regiment of Yorkshire

'Faithful'
Durham Light Infantry

'Firm'
WSFR, Worcestershire, 36th Foot

Sans peur
('Without fear')
93rd Highlanders

Merebimur
('We shall be worthy')
15/19 KRH, 15th King's Hussars

Pristinae virtutis memores
('Mindful of former valour')
8th King's Royal Irish Hussars

TOWERING BLACKPOOL

Blackpool Tower is 158m (518ft) high and was opened on 14 May 1894. More than 5 million bricks, 2,540 tonnes (2,800 tons) of steel and 94.5 tonnes (104 tons) of cast steel were used in its construction.

SOME TRADITIONAL PUB GAMES

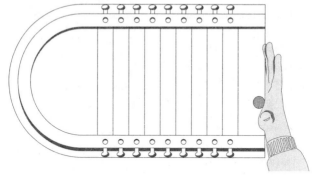

Western Skittles, Old English Skittles, Long Alley, Rolly Polly, Hood Skittles, Daddlums, Table Skittles (Devil Amongst the Tailors), The Long Game, The Northern Game, Horseshoe Pitching, The East Anglian Game, Indoor Quoits, Rings, Caves, Shoffe-Groat, Push Penny, Slide-thrift, Shove Ha'penny, Cribbage, Puff and Dart, East End Darts, Northern Darts, Stoolball, Bat and Trap, Knur and Spell, Cricket.

THE 50 MOST POPULAR PUB NAMES IN THE UK

1 Crown	18 Black Horse	35 Three Horseshoes
2 Red Lion	19 Prince of Wales	36 George and Dragon
3 Royal Oak	20 Victoria	37 Nag's Head
4 Swan	21 Greyhound	38 Globe
5 White Hart	22 Cross Keys	39 Fox
6 Railway	23 Star	40 Lamb
7 Plough	24 White Lion	41 Golden Lion
8 White Horse	25 Castle	42 Mason's Arms
9 Bell	26 Rising Sun	43 White Swan
10 New Inn	27 Anchor	44 Beehive
11 Ship	28 Chequers	45 Green Man
12 King's Head	29 Sun	46 Traveller's Rest
13 George	30 Bull	47 Foresters Arms
14 King's Arms	31 Coach and Horses	48 Waggon and Horses
15 Rose and Crown	32 Fox and Hounds	49 Black Bull
16 Wheatsheaf	33 Angel	50 Cricketers
17 Queens Head	34 Hare and Hounds	

A GUIDE TO BRITISH BEER-DRINKING TERMS

Ale A beer brewed with a top-fermenting yeast. It used to refer to a beer made without hops but this is not the case now.

Brown ale A bottled, lightly hopped and sweetish mild ale. Usually lower in gravity, though there are exceptions.

Cask Generic term for what most people would call a beer barrel.

Fining The process of clearing the beer by adding 'finings'. The finings act to clump together fine particles so they fall to the bottom of the cask. They consists of a thick liquid derived from seaweed or fish bladders, which precipitate fine particles.

Firkin A 41 litre (10.8 gallon) cask.

Free house A pub that is not bound by any agreements to sell any particular brewer's products.

Guest ale A beer from another brewery.

Hand pump Bar-mounted hand pull (not a tiny tap or connected to one). The handle is connected to a piston, which draws beer from the cask along a pipe to the spout.

Keg Pasteurised, filtered and artificially fizzed-up beer.

Mild A lightly hopped beer, often dark in colour and usually low in strength but high in flavour, mild was the preferred drink of workers in industrial Britain, who gulped gallons of the stuff as a restorative after long hours in coalmines, iron foundries and other sweaty sites.

Porter A dark and sweetish, but well-hopped beer.

Spiling For transit and storage, a cask is sealed, and a vent hole is provided on the top of the cask. Some while before being served, the peg that seals this hole (the spile hole), is knocked through to open up the beer to the atmosphere.

Ullage Waste beer left at the bottom of an empty cask or overflowing into a drip tray. It should not be filtered back into the cask. Most brewers allow for a proportion of 'lost' beer.

JACK THE RIPPER

Never identified or caught, he killed at least five women around London's East End in 1888.

A–Z OF ESSEX ENGLISH

arst past tense of 'ask'

bave to wash oneself

choona an edible fish purchased in a tin and usually prepared with mayonnaise

danstez on the ground floor

ejog a small, spiky animal

fantin jet of water for drinking or ornament

grand football stadium

haitch letter of the alphabet between g and i

ibeefa the Spanish holiday island

Jafta? Do you have to?

kaffy girl's name

levva material made from the skin of an animal

maffs the study of numbers

Nartamean? Do you know what I mean?

oaf a solemn declaration of truth or commitment

pans an annsis Imperial weight system

qualidee good

roofless without compassion

seevin very angry

tan ass modern terraced house

ump upset, as in 'get the ump'

vacher a document which can be exchanged for goods or services.

wannd up tense

yafta you have to

zaggerate suggest something is better or bigger than is true

UK EARTHQUAKES WITH A MAGNITUDE OF 4.5 ON THE RICHTER SCALE SINCE 1901

1901 Inverness	1944 Skipton
1903 Derby, Caernarvon	1957 Derby
1906 Swansea	1976 Widnes
1916 Stafford	1979 Carlisle
1926 Channel Islands, Ludlow	1984 Lleyn Peninsula
1927 Channel Islands	1990 Bishop's Castle
1931 Dogger Bank	1992 Roermond

HISTORY OF ENGLISH PLACE NAMES

Roman terms 50 BC to AD 410

Caster	fort, camp; town
cester	fort; camp; town
chester	fort, camp; town
fos(s)	ditch
port	harbour, gate
street	paved way

Celtic terms 800 BC to AD 400

aber	river mouth or ford
afon	river
allt	hillside
avon	river
bedd	grave
bont	bridge
bre	hill
bryn	hill, head
caer	fortress
capel	chapel
carnedd	cairn
castell	castle
coed	wood
cwm	valley
dee	river
dinas	city
don	hill
drum	hill
esk	river
eye	river
glan	river bank
hamps	dry stream in summer
llan	church
llyn	lake
mawr	big
môr	sea
mynydd	mountain
pant	hollow
pen	hill, head
plas	palace
pont	bridge
porth	harbour

HISTORY OF ENGLISH PLACE NAMES (CONT'D)

tre	hamlet, village, town
treath	beach
ynys	island

Saxon Terms AD 350 to 1000

bourne	stream
burg	large village
burn	stream
croft	small enclosure
cot	small hut
delph	ditch, dyke or stream
den(n)	pig pasture
ea, eg, eig, ey	island
fall	area cleared of trees
fen	fen
field	field
ham	village
hurst	clearing
ing	people
lake	lake
lea, ley	clearing
mere	pool
moor	moor
moss	swamp
riding	rod, cleared land
stead	place
stoc	summer pasture
stoke	'daughter' settlement
stow	holy place
ton, tun	house farm
weald	wold, high woodland
wic, wike	farm, group of huts
wood	wood
worth	fenced land
worthy	enclosed land

Viking Terms AD 750 to 1100

Akr	acre
beck	stream
booth	summer pasture
by	farm, village

ey	island
fell	hill or mound
fiord	fiord
fiskr	fish
gardr	yard, landing place
garth	enclosure
gate	road
geit	goat
gill	ravine or valley
holm(r)	island
how	hill or mound
hus	house
ings	marsh, meadow
kald	cold
kelda	spring, stream
kirk	church
laithe	barn
lin	flax
lund	grove
melr	sandbank
orme	serpent
pollr	pool
skar	cleft
sker	rock
slack	stream in a valley
stakkr	rock in the sea
stan	stone
stokkr	sound
tarn	lake
thorp	daughter settlement
thwaite	forest clearing, meadow
toft	homestead
wath	ford
wray	remote place

BRITAIN'S OLDEST MAN

Britain's oldest man was Bill Lee, from Stoke-on-Trent, who died in 2000 at the age of 108. He left behind his 98-year-old brother Tom, his 100-year-old sister Elsie, four grandchildren, ten great-grandchildren and two great-great grandsons.

YORKSHIRE'S TOP VISITOR ATTRACTIONS (PAID)

Attraction	Location	Visitors in 2002
Flamingo Land Theme Park and Zoo	Kirby Misperton	Around 1,393,000
The Deep	Hull	Around 750,000
Harewood House	Harewood	357,820
Cannon Hall Open Farm	Cawthorne	Around 350,000
Dalby Forest Drive and Visitor Centre	Low Dalby	330,981
Magna	Rotherham	291,143
North Yorkshire Moors Railway	Pickering	Around 290,000

BLING BLING

Terms that have their origins in black rap culutre:

bling bling originally meant 'ostentatious, flashy jewellery'; now describes a lifestyle of glitz and wealth
crib your home
Cris Cristal champagne
deep/dope great
diss disrespect
dreck used to describe poor quality
EZ pronounced 'easy', means 'fine'
fly cool, attractive
flava music with a bit of a Caribbean feel
gravy good
hangin' chilling with your homies (pals)
hoodie hooded jacket favoured by hip-hoppers
ice diamonds
jack to steal something
kickin' lively
phat/fat used to show approval, especially of someone or something that is fashionable, interesting or attractive
whacked out of control

THE POPULATION OF GREATER LONDON

7.93 million

WAX WOMAN

Madame Tussaud's in Marylebone Road, London, was founded by the aforementioned Frenchwoman, who learned her trade making grisly death masks of victims of the French Revolution.

ISLANDS OFF THE UK COAST

Alderney, Anglesey (Ynys Môn, Sir Yns Môn), Arran, Bardsey Island (Ynys Enlii), Barra, Benbecula (Beinn na Faoghla), Coll, Colonsay, Eigg, Eriskay, Guernsey, Harris, Herm, Iona, Islay, Isle of Man, Isle of Wight, Isles of Scilly (Scilly Isles, Scilly Islands, Scillies – 140 or so islands), Jersey, Jethou, Jura, Lewis (Isle of Lewis), Mull, North Uist, Orkney Islands (70 or so islands), Raasay, Rockall, Rum (Rhum), St Kilda, Sark, Sheppey, Shetland Islands (100 or so islands), Skye, South Uist, Staffa, Taransay, Tiree.

OOPS FIDO!

Rottweillers are the UK's most accident-prone dogs: nearly three in five need veterinary treatment during their lives. (One in five is the average across dog breeds).

THE GREAT EXHIBITION

The events leading up to the Great Exhibition of 1851 were prompted by the success of the French Industrial Exposition of 1844, when it was suggested to the English government that it would be most advantageous to British industry to have a similar exhibition in London. The building which housed the exhibition (known as the Crystal Palace) was designed by Thomas Paxton. The whole building was enormous – 563m (1,848ft) long and 124m (408ft) wide, with an extra bit sticking out on one side that measured 285m (936ft) by 14.6m (48ft). The central transept was 22m (72ft) wide and 33m (108ft) high, and a grand avenue and upstairs galleries ran the whole length of the building. Altogether, 71,791 sq m (772,758 sq ft) were roofed over, not including the 20,169 sq m (217,100 sq ft) of galleries. This was an area four times that of St Peter's in Rome, and six times that of St Paul's Cathedral. The total enclosed volume was 93,400 cubic m (33 million cubic ft). Materials included 559 tonnes (616 tons) of wrought iron, 3,556 tonnes (3,920 tons) of cast iron, 275,000m (900,000ft) of glass and 180,000m (600,000ft) of wooden planking to walk on. There were 323km (202 miles) of sash bars and 48km (30 miles) of gutters.

BRITAIN'S OLDEST WOMAN

Charlotte Hughes died at the age of 115 on 17 March 1993, at St David's Nursing Home in Redcar, Cleveland. She lived in her own home until 1991, when she began to have trouble walking. She kept her mental faculties until the very end. At the time of her death, she was not only the oldest person in Britain, but the second oldest person in the world.

PET CRAZY

People in Britain own more than 14.5 million dogs and cats. Pet owners are also spending nearly £3.5 billion ($5.8 billion) a year on their animals. The figure has gone up by almost 25 per cent in five years. Researchers found that most of the money spent goes on pet food, accessories and services such as grooming.

SHRINKING BRITAIN

The southern half of the British coastline is slowly sinking (on the east coast, at the rate of 5mm a year), while the northern half is rising, as a result of rebounding of the landmass, responding to the removal of ice from the last Ice Age. Some areas may be eroding at a rate of 6m (20ft) per year, but the current opinion is to surrender the land to the sea rather than build costly sea defences in rural areas. In 1996, it was reported that, as a result of tidal battering, 29 villages had disappeared from the Yorkshire coast in the previous 70 years.

BASS ROCK

Bass Rock is a volcanic islet in the Firth of Forth. It is about 107m (350ft) high, and has a ruined castle, as well as a chapel and a lighthouse. It is a seabird sanctuary, home to the third largest gannetry in the world and the largest one in Britain. Bass Rock's 16th-century castle was converted, after 1671, by the English government into a state prison, in which several eminent Covenanters were confined. The Rock was captured in 1691 and held until 1694 for James II by 16 Jacobites, against a small army of William III. St Baldred's chapel dates from the 15th century. The rock can be visited on summer excursions from North Berwick.

SAY WHAT?

The only two countries in the European Union without an official second language are England and Portugal.

YE OLDE ENGLISH ALPHABET

a b c d e f g h i k l m n o p q r

s s s t u w x y y   z æ ∂ þ   pæt and um

THE HISTORY OF THE UK'S MOST POPULAR DOG

In 1822, a traveller to Newfoundland gave an account of a number of small water dogs that waterfowlers preferred to use for retrieving because their smooth, short coats did not retain icy water in the freezing weather. The Earl of Malmesbury, upon seeing the swift, black dogs, took a liking to them and arranged to have some imported to England. It wasn't until 1887 that the name 'Labrador' was coined, when the earl incorrectly referred to them in a letter as his 'Labrador dog'. It was in the same letter that he also mentions the physical attributes that still distinguish the breed today: 'its close coat which turns the water off like oil and above all, a tail like an otter'.

LIGHTHOUSE BUILDERS OF BRITAIN

The modern method of building lighthouse towers came into favour when Smeaton completed the second Eddystone Lighthouse in 1759. It was made of massive blocks of stone, dovetailed together, with the foundations being dovetailed into the rock itself, so the lighthouse really became a continuation of the rock on which it was built. Also, the shape of the tower (tapering towards the top) was based on the principle of the tree trunk, which weathers storms so efficiently. There are, of course, different plans and designs for dovetailing the stonework, but the principle of Smeaton is still used today. The walls are made much thicker at the bottom of the lighthouse than at the top, and in the Wolf Rock Lighthouse, off Land's End, for instance, the walls at the level of the entrance door are nearly 2.5m (8ft) thick, and gradually decrease until they are only 69cm (27in) near the top.

AWWIGHT ME OLD CHINAS? SOME TRADITIONAL COCKNEY RHYMING SLANG

Adam and Eve – believe

almond rocks – socks

apples and pears – stairs

Aristotle – bottle

Ascot races – braces

baked bean – Queen

baker's dozen – cousin

ball and chalk – walk

barnet fair – hair

battle cruiser – boozer

boat race – face

Bob Hope – soap

boracic lint – skint

Brahms and Liszt – pissed

brass tacks – facts

bread and honey – money

bricks and mortar – daughter

brown bread – dead

bubble and squeak – Greek

butcher's hook – look

Chalk Farm – arm

china plate – mate

currant bun – sun

daisy roots – boots

Darby and Joan – moan

Dicky bird – word

dicky dirt – shirt

dinky doos – shoes

dog and bone – phone

dustbin lid – kid

frog and toad – road

Gregory Peck – neck

Hank Marvin – starving

jam jar – car

Aunt Joanna – piano

Khyber Pass – arse

kick and prance – dance

Lady Godiva – fiver

loaf of bread – head

mince pies – eyes

north and South – mouth

oily rag – fag

pen and ink – stink

plates of meat – feet

pony and trap – crap

porky pies – lies

Rosie Lee – tea

round the houses – trousers

rub-a-dub – rub

Ruby Murray – curry

skin and blister – sister

sky rocket – pocket

syrup of figs – wigs

tea Leaf – thief

titfer tat – hat

trouble and strife – wife

whistle and flute – suit

BRITAIN'S OLDEST PORT

Poole Harbour is Britain's oldest working cross-channel port. Archaeologists found ancient piles (wooden supports) dating back to 250 BC within a series of jetties at the harbour. Two jetties have been found: one projecting southwest from Green Island, and the other northeast from Cleavel Point.

DRY-STONE WALLS

Mortarless stone walls are a common sight in Britain. In upland farming areas, these dry-stone walls often replace hedges and fences as field boundaries, and typically consist of an outer layer of large stones concealing a core of smaller ones. Dry-stone walling is an ancient skill, and not only are there various different styles of stone wall around the UK, but different stones are used according to what can be found naturally in the area. For example, Cotswold dry-stone walling usually consists of Oolitic limestone, which is relatively soft and easily worked, and creates walls that are tightly packed and neatly finished with smaller stones. Cornwall sees the heavy use of slate, and walls are often constructed in a herringbone pattern. The infill between the slate is usually earth, which accounts for the flowers and grasses that can often be seen growing from Cornish walls. Derbyshire walls tend to be more irregular, due to the coarse sandstone, which is difficult to work into even blocks. Likewise, North Yorkshire stone walls are often irregular, while those in South Yorkshire are more even and compactly bonded.

THE STORY OF MORRIS DANCING

The Morris dance is a ritual folk dance performed in rural England, originally by groups of men. Once linked with the pagan fertility rites of spring, the dance is performed wearing bright costumes, handkerchiefs and bells, and often represents a folk tale. The word 'Morris' possibly derived from morisco or from the Middle English moreys (meaning 'Moorish'). There are three main traditions: Cotswold Morris (performed with sticks and hankies), Northwest Morris (processional, wearing clogs) and Border Morris (from the Welsh borders, and is performed in blackface, with a vigorous clashing of sticks).

COME TO GLOUCESTER

Gloucestershire has 1 per cent of England's population on 2 per cent of its area. More than half (54 per cent) of the county's area is in an Area of Outstanding Natural Beauty or Green Belt, and only 5 per cent is urbanised.

BRITAIN'S MAIN WALKS

The West Highland Way

Stretching 153km (95 miles) from Milngavie near Glasgow to north of Fort William, the West Highland Way takes in some of the most spectacular scenery in Britain. It even goes to the foot of Britain's highest mountain, Ben Nevis, and also follows the shores of Loch Lomond, Scotland's largest loch.

The Pennine Way

Britain's first designated Long Distance Path stretches for 410km (256 miles) from Edale in Derbyshire along the Pennine mountain chain, and finishes at Kirk Yetholm on the Scottish border. Hill, mountain and moorland scenery is occasionally broken up with an inn perched on the path. Notable parts of the path include: at 636m (2,088ft), Kinder Scout in Derbyshire; the 893m (2,930ft) Cross Fell in Cumbria, Pen-y-Ghent in the Yorkshire Dales; Tan Hill Inn; and Wishields Crag in Northumberland, where the path crosses Hadrian's Wall.

Coast to Coast walk

The Coast to Coast walk is a popular route for those raising money for charity, extending 306km (190 miles) across the Lake District, Yorkshire Dales and North York Moors, and covering spectacular mountain and moorland scenery. Those that have walked its full length recommend walking west to east to take advantage of prevailing winds.

Offa's Dyke

Offa's Dyke runs for 270km (168 miles) of varying scenery, from valleys to moorland and mountains, and follows the Welsh border with England, passing through the Brecon Beacons National Park. Offa's Dyke is a defensive earthwork dyke along the Welsh border, of which there are remains from the mouth of the River Dee to that of the Severn.

Icknield Way

Major pre-Roman trackway traversing southeast England. It runs from Wells-next-the-Sea on the Norfolk coast in a generally southwesterly direction, passing first through Cambridgeshire and Hertfordshire to the source of the River Kennet in Wiltshire. It covers 168km (105 miles).

North Downs Way

The North Downs run from Andover (on the edge of Salisbury Plain) in the west to the cliffs of South Foreland in the east. The North Downs Way is 226km (141 miles) long.

Cotswold Way
This path follows the escarpment of the Cotswold hills, and is 163km (102 miles) long. It starts at Bath and ends up at Chipping Campden, Gloucestershire.

Hadrian's Wall Path
Only about 16km (10 miles) of the original wall – running from the Solway Firth in the west to the to the Tyne mouth in the east – are still standing, although earthworks make it possible to trace the route for 117km (73 miles).

Southwest Coastal Path
Starting at Minehead in Somerset, the Southwest Coastal Path covers 965km (600 miles) of spectacular coastal scenery around the West Country peninsula, ending at Poole Harbour in Dorset.

Isle of Wight Coastal Path
Chalk cliffs, downs and deep ravines, known locally as 'chines', are all part of the Isle of Wight Coastal Path. The route circles the entire island on a 104km (65 mile) footpath.

South Downs Way
The chalk hills running from near Petersfield, Hampshire, across Sussex to the south coast at Beachy Head near Eastbourne are called the South Downs. Facing the North Downs across the Weald, they are used as sheep pasture. The South Downs Way traverses the area for 170km (106 miles) – from Winchester, Hampshire to Eastbourne, East Sussex.

The Thames Path
The Thames rises at Kemble (near Cirencester) in the Cotswold Hills, and follows a course of 341km (213 miles) to the Nore, where it flows into the North Sea.

The Ridgeway
The Ridgeway is the grassy track, dating from prehistoric times, that runs along the Berkshire Downs from Avebury in Wiltshire to Ivinghoe Beacon in Buckinghamshire. The path covers 136km (85 miles) of Berkshire, Oxfordshire and the Chilterns.

Pennine Bridleway
Work is currently under way to create a northern extension of the Pennine Bridleway. This would take the route through Cumbria into Northumberland, ending at Byrness in the Kielder Forest Park, just south of the Scottish border. Starting at Carsington Reservoir or Middleton Top, Derbyshire, it finishes 330km (206 miles) later at Fat Lamb Inn, Kirkby Stephen, Cumbria.

BRITAIN'S MAIN WALKS (CONT'D)

Wolds Way and Cleveland Way

The Wolds Way begins at Hessle Haven, in the shadow of the Humber Bridge. It winds its way through 128 km (79 miles) of chalk countryside, which runs first north from the Humber and then east, to terminate in the 122m (400ft) cliffs of Bempton, at the dramatic outcrop of Filey Brigg. The path continues northwards, then becoming the 174km (109 mile) Cleveland Way, following the coastline past Robin Hood's Bay and Whitby. Then it continues virtually around the border of the North York Moors National Park boundary and ends at the delightful market town of Helmsley, North Yorkshire.

SOME FASCINATING FACTS ABOUT PURBECK IN DORSET

The name 'Purbeck' comes from Purbik, meaning 'a beak-shaped ridge frequented by bittern or snipe'.

Purbeck is one of the richest districts for wildlife in Dorset.

Purbeck has over 200 species and 30 habitats of conservation concern.

The entire coastline is a World Heritage Site and Heritage Coast.

Internationally important fossils, including dinosaur footprints, have been found in Purbeck.

England's longest National Trail is the South West Coast Path, which starts in Purbeck.

There is 333km (208 miles) of running water in Purbeck, including the rivers Frome and Piddle.

Purbeck's rivers and wetlands attract over 30,000 wintering waterbirds.

Purbeck has 5 per cent of England's reed-beds.

52km (33 miles) of hard coast support 40,000 waterbirds in the winter.

Purbeck plays host to 80 per cent of the south coast's puffins.

The coast supports Purbeck's endemic rock sea lavender, bottle-nosed dolphins, breeding sandwich and common terns, and the UK's first breeding little egrets.

Durlston Country Park, near Swanage, is one of the best places to spot dolphins in the UK.

Poole Harbour, of which the majority falls in the Purbeck district, is the second largest in the world and is now the world's largest natural harbour.

Purbeck is home to over half of the UK sand lizard population.

SOME THINGS JUST NEVER CHANGE

In 1901, the average speed of traffic in London was 12mph (19kph), and the figure remains the same 100 years later. The proportion of the nation's population living in London has remained at 12 per cent over the same period as well. Spooky…

ARTHUR'S TABLE?

The large Round Table hanging in the Great Hall of Winchester Cathedral is supposed to have belonged to King Arthur and his bold knights. Unfortunately, forensic tests have dated it as being built in around 1335 – some 700 years after Arthur lived!

THE GLORIOUS TWELFTH

The traditional grouse season runs from 12 August (known as the 'Glorious Twelfth') until 10 December, but the birds are best in the first half of the season. There are many species of this game bird but the red Scottish grouse reputedly has the best flavour. It can be found feeding on heather moors in Scotland, Ireland and northern parts of England, and it is the heather that gives the meat its gamey richness. Young grouse are best if roasted, then covered with rashers of bacon to protect them from drying out. Serve with game chips (home-made potato crisps, really thinly sliced) and watercress, as is common with other game birds. Grouse can also be used to make game pie, or braised slowly in wine and stock with celery and onions for a truly seasonal dish.

KING GEORGE: THE SEQUEL

The movie *The Madness Of King George* was originally released in England under the title of *The Madness Of King George III*. The 'III' was dropped for its American release, however, because it was believed that the American moviegoer would think it was a sequel, and not go and see it because they had not yet seen *The Madness Of King George I* and *II*!

WORK THIS ONE OUT

Gravesend is 42km (26 miles) away from London by river, but only 38km (24 miles) away by land.

SOME MOVIE BLOCKBUSTERS SHOT IN SCOTLAND

Local Hero (1983)
Filmed in Pennan, this delightful 1983 comedy has a red phone box at the centre of the plot, which still attracts fans to this little village in the northeast of Scotland.

Loch Ness (1994)
Filmed on Loch Ness, this romantic comedy brings American star Ted Danson and British actress Joely Richardson together in search of Nessie.

Rob Roy (1994)
Filmed in Perthshire, it starred Liam Neeson (as the Highland folk hero Rob Roy MacGregor) and Jessica Lange (as his wife).

Shallow Grave (1994)
Filmed in Glasgow and Edinburgh, this home-grown thriller starring Ewan McGregor shows three friends spiralling into madness as they conceal a corpse for profit.

Braveheart (1995)
Filmed in Glencoe and Glen Nevis, this starred Mel Gibson as the Scottish hero William Wallace – he who fought to drive the English from Scotland in the 13th century.

Mary Reilly (1996)
Filmed in Edinburgh Old Town, *Mary Reilly* starred Julia Roberts as the maid of Dr Jekyll and his sinister alter ego, Mr Hyde.

BRITAIN'S MOST PROLIFIC MURDERERS

Fred and Rose West
Between 1968 and 1987, Fred West killed 13 women and girls – including his first wife and two of his daughters – in Gloucester and nearby Much Marcle. His wife Rose, who is serving a life sentence in London's Holloway prison, was convicted of 10 of the murders. Fred hanged himself in Birmingham's Winson Green prison on New Year's Day 1995.

Dr Harold Shipman
Dr Shipman was found guilty at Preston Crown Court of the murder of 15 of his patients, but it is thought he may be responsible for the deaths of around 150 more.

Mary Anne Cotton
Convicted of six murders in 1873, Cotton is widely held to have sent more than 20 victims to an early grave. Across a 20-year period, her life was marked by determined efforts to scale the social ladder and by the number

of husbands, children and relatives who died (of remarkably similar symptoms) in her presence.

Dennis Nilsen

Nilsen claimed to have killed 16 young men between 1978 and 1983. He lured them back to his flat in Muswell Hill, north London, before mutilating them.

Peter Sutcliffe

Sutlcliffe, aka the Yorkshire Ripper, became the subject of one of the largest police manhunts during the 1970s and early 1980s as he preyed on women across the north of England. He later claimed that messages from God had driven him to murder his 13 victims.

John Haigh

Haigh was branded the 'acid bath vampire' after he claimed to drink the blood of the six victims he disposed of in vats of acid. He was hanged in 1949.

John Christie

In the 1940s, Christie's activities around 10 Rillington Place, west London, included gassing eight people and sexually interfering with their corpses. He was hanged in 1953.

Ken Erskine

The brutal murder of seven pensioners in south London saw Ken Erskine earn himself notoriety as the Stockwell Strangler. Motivated mainly by the desire to get his hands on his victims' money, Erskine was jailed for 40 years in 1988.

Ian Brady and Myra Hindley

The Moors Murderers killed five small children, whom they disposed of on Manchester's bleak Saddleworth Moor in the 1960s. Brady is still in jail, but Hindley died in 2002.

Dr John Bodkin Adams

Echoing Harold Shipman's activities (above), Bodkin Adams was acquitted in 1953 of the murder of an elderly widow in Eastbourne. However, since his death further evidence has emerged to suggest he may have helped up to 25 of his patients into their graves, but not before 'encouraging' them to name him in their wills.

AN ALTERNATIVE DARWIN THEORY

Naturalist Charles Darwin was told not to pen his ground-breaking book *On The Origin of Species* (1859) because it was too boring. He was advised to write about pigeons instead.

THE POET LAUREATE

In Great Britain, the Poet Laureate is:

• the realm's official poet

• a member of the royal household

• charged with writing verses for court and national occasions (such as for a royal wedding or the New Year)

• awarded the position for life

• chosen by the British reigning monarch, from a list of nominees that the prime minister compiles after a poet laureate dies

THE GREAT STINK

The Thames used to be incredibly dirty because it was where all London's waste ended up. In 1858, the stench became so bad it was known as 'The Great Stink', so plans were drawn up to provide proper sewers and drainage. The Victoria Embankment between Westminster and Blackfriars bridges houses some of these, providing a major route from Westminster to the City.

YORKSHIRE'S TOP VISITOR ATTRACTIONS (FREE)

Attraction	Location	Visitors in 2002
York Minster	York	Around 1,570,500
National Museum of Photography, Film & Television	Bradford	Around 795,371
National Railway Museum	York	742,515
Lotherton Hall Estate	Aberford	Around 650,000
Brymor Ice Cream Parlour	Masham	Around 322,000
Royal Armouries Museum	Leeds	280,000
Leeds City Art Gallery	Leeds	233,330
Jorvik Glass	York	191, 058
Bronte Weaving Shed	Haworth	148,905

SHIPPING FORECAST AREAS

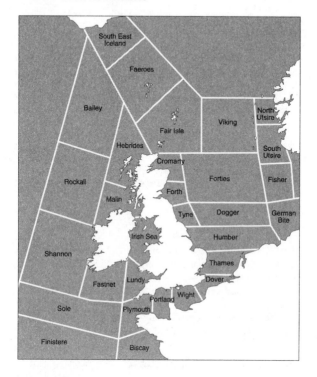

SILENT NIGHT?

Snoring is the second most irritating bed habit after duvet hogging. Over five million people in the UK snore each night.

SAXON SCHEME

The bodies of 650 excavated Saxons are to have burials, paid for by an 'Adopt-a-Skeleton' scheme.

ROYAL TATTOO

King George V acquired his first tattoo aboard HMS *Baccante* – from the famous Japanese tattooist Hori Chyo.

BURKE AND HARE

William Burke and William Hare lived in Edinburgh in 1828. They were Irish labourers, who lodged with local prostitutes Maggie Laird and Nell MacDougal. Maggie let rooms out to the public and, one day, when one of her lodgers died, Burke and Hare saw an opportunity to make money and sold the corpse to local anatomist Dr Knox. Soon enough, the two were in business supplying corpses by means of grave robbery. Dr Knox's demand for bodies for dissection exceeded their regular supply, so they then took to murder. Receiving a handsome price for every corpse, their motive was pure gain.

In the next nine months they murdered 16 people. They were finally caught out and brought to justice: Burke and Nell MacDougal were tried, Hare and Maggie Laird turned king's evidence. Nell won a verdict of not proven, while Burke was found guilty and sentenced to death, and was hanged at Edinburgh on 28 January 1829 before a large crowd.

NOT A DROP TO DRINK

When the sun came out over London's Mile End on 4 March 1893, nobody guessed that it would not rain again for more than two months. At 73 days, this drought was the longest on record. The summer of 2003 saw Britain's highest ever temperature (37.2°C (98.96°F) at Heathrow Airport) which beat the previous record of 37.1°C (98.8°F), noted in Cheltenham in 1990. The lowest temperature is comfortably the bone-chilling −27.2°C (−17°F), recorded at Braemar in Scotland in 1982.

THE MODERN-DAY BEAUFORT SCALE

Beaufort number	Wind Speed (knots)	World Meteorological Organization description	Sea state	Wave Height (metres)
0	0–1	Calm	Calm; like a mirror	0
1	2–3	Light air	Ripples with appearance of scales: no foam crests	0.1
2	4–6	Light breeze	Small wavelets; crests of glassy appearance, not breaking	0.2–0.3

3	7–10	Gentle breeze	Large wavelets; crests begin to break; scattered whitecaps	0.6–1
4	11–16	Moderate breeze	Small waves, becoming longer numerous whitecaps	1–1.5
5	17–21	Fresh breeze	Moderate waves, taking longer form; many whitecaps; some spray	2–2.5
6	22–27	Strong breeze	Larger waves forming; whitecaps everywhere; more spray	3–4
7	28–33	Near gale	Sea heaps up; white foam from breaking waves begins to be blown in streaks	4–5.5
8	34–40	Gale	Moderately high waves of greater length; edges of crests begin to break into spindrift; foam is blown in well-marked streaks	6–7.5
9	41–47	Strong gale	High waves; sea begins to roll; dense streaks of foam; spray may reduce visibility	7–10
10	48–55	Storm	Very high waves with overhanging crests; sea takes white appearance as foam is blown in very dense streaks; rolling is heavy and visibility is reduced	9–12.5
11	56–63	Violent storm	Exceptionally high waves; sea covered with white foam patches; visibility still more reduced	11.5–16
12	> 64	Hurricane	Air filled with foam; sea completely white with driving spray; visibility greatly reduced	14–16

IPSWICH OR GIPESWIC?

Back in AD 993, Ipswich was known as Gipeswic, and meant 'Gip's port or landing place'.

PUB TRIV

The word 'pub' is a shortened form of 'public house', for at one time alehouses were private homes where the occupant brewed ale and sold it at the front door. Poles topped with evergreen branches were hung outside public houses so customers could easily find them; these were the earliest pub signs. Today there is an amazing selection of pub names depicted on colourful signs hanging above the door, and these often refer to historical events or local landmarks or characters. Other pub names refer to animals, many with their origins in heraldry, such as the White Hart and the Red Lion (said to be the most common name of all).

BRITAIN'S MOST DANGEROUS A ROADS

Based on the number of fatal and serious vehicle accidents per 1 billion kilometres (625 million miles) travelled between 1997 and 1999, these are the roads to watch:

A889	A86–A9 (near Dalwhinnie)
A537	Macclesfield–Buxton
A12	Romford-M25
A4137	A49–A40 (west of Ross-on-Wye)
A628	A616–Penistone
A1001	Hatfield
A534	Welsh boundary to Nantwich
A533	Runcorn–A56
A682	M65 Junction 13–A65 Long Preston
A13	(now A1306) Aveley A1306–M25

ABSOLUTELY BARMY

Madness were one of the most successful and best-loved British bands in the 1980s, with hits that included 'Baggy Trousers', 'Our House' and 'One Step Beyond'. For the cover of their 1980 album *Absolutely*, the Nutty Boys are pictured in their famous baggy trousers, outside London's Chalk Farm tube station.

THE GIANT'S CAUSEWAY

The Giant's Causeway, on the Antrim coast close to Bushmills, consists of a protrusion of basalt hexagonal columns jutting into the sea. According to scientific facts, the Causeway was formed 62–65 million years ago by the cooling of volcanic rock. Local legend leads us to believe, however, that the Causeway was built by two feuding giants – Finn MacCool in Ireland and Benandonner in Scotland – who needed to travel across the sea in order to do battle. The site was discovered by the Bishop of Derry in 1692, and attracts many visitors every year to see the estimated 40,000 columns.

OFFICE RAGE

51 per cent of UK employees think their office toilet is filthy all the time, while 4 per cent want their own personal toilet.

A medical instrument manufacturer in Scotland has demanded that its employees cut down on the amount they flush the toilet, limiting them to two flushes each per day.

A Cold War memorabilia company has recycled used ejection seats from old B-52 bombers, and made them into executive chairs. The perfect gift for an overbearing boss?

A recent study found that there are 400 times more bacteria on your desk than on the average toilet.

The biggest complaint amongst co-workers is unreturned emails and phone calls.

CHOCOLATE TOWN

After the successful move of the Cadbury Brothers' chocolate factory to Bournville, near Birmingham, George Cadbury decided to build a garden village next to it. He was spurred on by the dreadful conditions he saw in the slums of Birmingham, and started to develop a small community with well-planned houses and big gardens. The first 57 hectares (140 acres) were purchased in 1895, and 143 cottages were built. Houses of different sizes were built together to create a mixture of small and large families, and by the turn of the 20th century there were 313 houses on 134 hectares (330 acres). Gradually the heart of the village grew around the village green – the shops, school and other community buildings. On 14 December 1900, George Cadbury set up the Bournville Village Trust to maintain and develop the estate, which it continues to do today.

GHERKIN, ANYONE?

The Swiss Re Building in the City of London is the latest addition to the capital's skyline. The 41-storey-high, round, tapered building was designed by Lord Norman Foster and its shape has earned it the sobriquet of 'The Exotic Gherkin'. Its construction involved the levelling of the old Baltic Exchange building, which was severely damaged by an IRA bomb in 1992.

THE GUNPOWDER PLOT

In 1505, a group of Catholic conspirators including Robert Catesby, Thomas Winter, Thomas Percy, John Wright and Guy Fawkes, a siege expert who had worked for the Spanish in Flanders, decided to wipe out the Houses of Parliament by planting 36 barrels of gunpowder in a cellar beneath the old Westminster Hall. The plot was scheduled for 5 November, but was foiled the night before. New research suggests that had the explosion gone off, it would have caused total destruction in a radius of 135ft – destroying the old Palace of Westminster, Westminster Hall, the Abbey and surrounding streets.

Today the 'Gunpowder Plot' is celebrated every 5 November with fireworks and bonfires. A dummy of Fawkes is traditionally wheeled through the streets, with the cry 'Penny for the Guy', before being thrown onto the flames.

SOME FASCINATING FACTS ABOUT THE QUEEN

During her reign the Queen has been given a seven-year-old elephant, a bull and two tortoises.

Since coming to the throne in 1952, she has given regular Tuesday evening audiences to 10 prime ministers and given Royal Assent to 3,135 Acts of Parliament.

The Queen has received around three million items of correspondence, conferred 380,000 honours and awards, and sent 37,000 Christmas cards in the past 50 years.

She has conducted 251 official visits overseas – to 128 different countries ranging from the Cocos Islands with a population of 655, to the People's Republic of China with a population of 1.25 billion.

Of these, Canada proved the most popular with Her Majesty. She has visited the country 19 times.

The Queen has sent 100,000 telegrams to centenarians and 280,000 to couples celebrating their diamond wedding anniversary in the UK and the Commonwealth.

During her reign, more than a million guests have attended garden parties at Buckingham Palace or the Palace of Holyroodhouse, Edinburgh.

She has given 88 state banquets.

Her Majesty has also launched 17 ships, attended 31 Royal Variety Performances, made 48 Christmas broadcasts and posed for more than 120 portraits since 1952.

She has owned more than 30 corgis since 1944 when she was given her first, Susan, as an 18th birthday present.

PHILIP THE GOD?

Prince Philip, the Duke of Edinburgh, is worshipped as a god on the island of Tanna, in Vanuatu in the south-west Pacific.

TALL TALES

As standards of living and nutrition have improved, the average Briton has got taller at the rate of 0.75 inches (1.9cm) a generation. Official Health Of The Nation figures show 30% of men under 25 are now over six feet tall. If the current trend continues the average British man's height will be 6ft (2.08m) within a couple of generations and the average woman will be nudging 5ft 7ins (1.62m).

Britain's tallest man is currently Chris Greener, who towers at 7ft 6ins (2.28m).

BAA HUMBUG

In Wales, there are more sheep than people. The population for Wales is 2,921,000 with approximately 5,000,000 sheep.

NUMBER OF PEOPLE IN PRISON IN THE UK IN 2003

74,149

WHAT A SAUCE!

HP Sauce is a popular brown sauce produced in Birmingham, England. It has a malt vinegar base blended with fruit and spices. The original recipe was invented and developed by FG Garton, a grocer from Nottingham. FG Garton's Sauce Manufacturing began to market HP Sauce in 1903. Garton came to call the sauce HP because he had heard that a restaurant in the Houses of Parliament had begun serving it. Garton sold the recipe and HP brand for the sum of £150 and the settlement of some unpaid bills to Edwin Samson Moore. HP Sauce became known as 'Wilson's Gravy' in the 1960s and '70s after Harold Wilson, the Labour Prime Minister who, it was alleged, used to cover his food with the sauce. The allegation was neither confirmed nor denied by Wilson.

TIME TO DIE: THE TOP 10 MOST COMMON CAUSES OF DEATH IN THE UK

Circulatory System Diseases
Cancers
Respiratory Diseases
Digestive Diseases
Injury and Poisoning
Nervous System and Sense Organs
Mental Disorders
Metabolic Disorders
Genito-Urinary Diseases
Infectious and Parasitic Diseases

DEATH IN THE AFTERNOON

Spencer Percival is the only British Prime Minister to have been assassinated. On the morning of 11 May 1811, Percival told his wife that he had dreamt the previous night that he was shot in the House of Commons by a man wearing a green coat with brass buttons. Despite the pleading of his family not to go to Parliament that day, Percival felt he had to attend as his Premiership was being questioned due to current conduct of the Peninsula Campaign. At about 5pm that afternoon he was leaving the House of Commons chamber when John Bellingham, a disaffected servant of the Crown from Liverpool approached from behind some folding-doors and fired one shot at Percival which hit him in the chest, killing him instantly. Bellingham was found guilty of murder and sentenced to death by hanging. On 18 May 1811 (seven days after Percival's shooting), he was executed in front of Newgate Prison.

BRITAIN'S BIGGEST ROBBERIES

1963: The Great Train Robbery

On 8 August 1963 armed robbers stole £2.6 million ($4.4 million), mostly in used bank notes, from a Glasgow–London Royal Mail train, near Bridego Bridge north of London. Six people were hired to burn down their farmhouse hideout, but did such a poor job that the police found everyone's fingerprints. With this and other evidence, 12 of the 15 robbers were caught, convicted and jailed.

1983: Britain's Biggest Cash Robbery

Almost £6 million ($10 million) was stolen from the Security Express headquarters in Shoreditch, east London, in 1983. Ronnie Knight, the former husband of actress Barbara Windsor, was jailed after admitting handling some of the proceeds. He denied taking part in the robbery. Knight was jailed after spending 10 years in Spain, where he fled the night his brother, John, was arrested in 1984. John Knight was jailed for 22 years.

1990: £292 million ($495 million) City Bonds Robbery

At 9:30am on 2 May 1990, John Goddard, a 58-year-old messenger with money broker Sheppards, was mugged at knifepoint on a quiet side street in the City of London. Mr Goddard was taking Bank of England Treasury bills and certificates of deposit from banks and building societies. The bonds were in bearer form and as good as cash to anyone holding them. Police believe the City mugging was carried out by Patrick Thomas, a petty crook from south London. Thomas was found dead from a gunshot wound to the head in December 1991. He was never charged with the robbery.

1996: The Hole-In-The-Wall Gang

A global conspiracy by an elite team of criminals to steal millions from cashpoint machines. Seven conspirators, from Kent and London, admitted their part in a plot which would have undermined the public's confidence in cash dispensers. The plan was discovered when a computer expert the gang tried to recruit went to the police. Police said it could have been the biggest theft in British history.

8 November 2000: The Millennium Dome Gang

Police foiled 'the robbery of the millennium' when they caught a gang smashing their way into the Millennium Dome with a JCB earthmover to snatch £200 million ($340 million) worth of diamonds. Four men were sentenced at the Old Bailey for conspiracy to rob. A fifth man was found guilty of the lesser charge of conspiracy to steal.

11 February 2000: The Heathrow Heist

A gang of thieves carried out a dramatic robbery at London's Heathrow airport, attacking the driver of a security van before escaping with an estimated £6.5 million ($11 million) in cash.

LUCKY LOTTO

On 2 January 2002, an anonymous player from Switzerland won
£16,627,894 ($24,168,450) on the UK Lotto. It is the largest cash prize
ever won by an individual player in UK Lotto's history. His winning numbers
were 2–6–20–24–29–32. The UK Lotto jackpot was not won on 26
December so the amount was 'rolled over' to 29 December 2001. It was
not won again and 'rolled over' to 2 January, when the player's numbers
came up. He was the only winner of the jackpot in that draw.

THE UK'S MOST POPULAR/UNPOPULAR CAR ACCORDING TO *WHICH? CAR* MAGAZINE

POPULAR	UNPOPULAR
BMW X5	Citroen Saxo
Toyota Yaris Verso	Citroen Xsara
Skoda Octavia	Peugeot 106
Mazda MX 5	Rover 25
Lexus IS200	Rover 45

TOP TEN DOG AND BITCH NAMES

	Male	Female
1	Max	Molly
2	Charlie	Holly
3	Ben	Rosie
4	Jake	Poppy
5	Barney	Lucy
6	Jack	Ellie
7	Buster	Tess
8	Toby	Meg
9	Jasper	Bonnie
10	Oscar	Daisy

MISSING MILLIONS

The largest unclaimed Lotto prize is £664,092 ($1,127,000). The ticket was bought in Southwark, south London on 24 September 2001, and the winning numbers were 2–25–34–35–36–39, with the Bonus 26. The biggest unclaimed prize which has since expired was £3 million ($5 million) on a ticket bought in Hull in 1996.

SOME QUOTES FROM MARGARET THATCHER

'To cure the British disease with socialism was like trying to cure leukaemia with leeches.'

'No woman in my time will be prime minister or chancellor or foreign secretary – not the top jobs. Anyway, I wouldn't want to be prime minister; you have to give yourself 100 per cent.'

'I am extraordinarily patient, provided I get my own way in the end.'

'Pennies do not come from heaven. They have to be earned here on earth.'

'A world without nuclear weapons would be less stable and more dangerous for all of us.'

'What is success? I think it is a mixture of having a flair for the thing that you are doing; knowing that it is not enough, that you have got to have hard work and a certain sense of purpose.'

'What Britain needs is an iron lady.'

'If you lead a country like Britain, a strong country, a country which has taken a lead in world affairs in good times and in bad, a country that is always reliable, then you have to have a touch of iron about you.'

DEFUNCT UK COINAGE

Farthing, halfpenny, silver threepence, groat, sixpence, shilling, florin, half a crown, crown, noble, sovereign, half-sovereign, guinea.

HOW TO CONTACT THE PRIME MINSTER

Email: via www.number-10.gov.uk

Writing: The Prime Minister, 10 Downing Street, London SW1A 2AA

Fax: 020 7925 0918. (From outside the UK, the number is +44 20 7925 0918)

ELEMENTARY: 10 BRITISH LITERARY SLEUTHS (AND THEIR CREATORS)

Miss Marple (Agatha Christie)

Inspector Rebus (Ian Rankin)

Inspector Morse (Colin Dexter)

Inspector Frost (RD Wingfield)

Dalziel and Pascoe (Reginald Hill)

Sherlock Holmes (Arthur Conan Doyle)

Commander Adam Dalgliesh (PD James)

Chief Inspector Wexford (Ruth Rendall)

Inspector Barnaby (Caroline Graham)

Inspector Alleyn (Ngaio Marsh)

FAMOUS NURSERY RHYMES – AND WHAT THEY WERE REALLY ABOUT

'Ring O' Roses' (Bubonic plague)

'Remember, Remember' (The Gunpowder Plot)

'Old Mother Hubbard' (Cardinal Wolsey and the Catholic Church)

'Georgie Porgie' (George, Duke of Buckingham)

'Humpty Dumpty' (an unusually large cannon which was mounted on the protective wall of St Mary's Wall Church in Colchester)

'Three Blind Mice' (three noblemen who were plotting against Mary, Queen of Scots)

'Old King Cole' (3rd century British king Godebog)

'Little Jack Horner' (the steward to the Bishop of Glastonbury in the 16th century)

'Ride a Cock Horse' (Elizabeth I)

'Who Killed Cock Robin' (Robin Hood)

THE DEADLY FLOOD

The floods on the night of 31 January 1953 were the worst peacetime disaster in Britain during the 20th century. What had begun as an unremarkable weather front far out in the Atlantic had turned into what meteorologists sometimes call 'the perfect storm'. As the piled-up waters from the Atlantic reached the North Sea, rising winds of well over 160kph (100mph) – and coming disastrously from the North – began to drive a wall of water down the North Sea.

Worse still, it coincided with high tide. In its path were dozens of unsuspecting coastal communities living in wooden prefabricated homes. More than 300 people died and thousands more were left homeless.

TEN GREAT BRITISH FOLLIES

The House in the Clouds, Suffolk

Portmeirion, Wales

Nore Folly, West Sussex

Wainhouse's Tower, West Yorkshire

The Tattingstone Wonder, Suffolk

The Rocket Ship, West Yorkshire

King Alfred's Tower, Wiltshire

The Pineapple, Scotland

The Temple of the Four Winds, North Yorkshire

Ilton Stonehenge, North Yorkshire

THE HANGMAN COMETH

Born in Bradford, West Yorkshire, in 1905, Albert Pierrepoint was by far the most prolific hangman of the 20th century, having executed an estimated 433 men and 17 women in his 24 years of service in Britain and abroad. He learned his trade assisting his uncle Tom and is credited with the quickest hanging on record when he executed James Inglis in only 7 seconds on 8 May 1951 at Strangeways in Manchester.

Pierrepoint died in his own bed in 1992.

THE RED MAP: FORMER BRITISH DOMINIONS, COLONIES, PROTECTORATES, PROTECTED AND ASSOCIATED STATES, MANDATED AND TRUST TERRITORIES FROM THE AGE OF EMPIRE

Aden

Antigua and Barbuda

Australia

Bahamas

Barbados

Basutoland

Bechuanaland

British Antarctic Territory

British Central Africa

British East Africa

British Guiana

British Honduras

British Indian Ocean Territory

British New Guinea (Papua)

British Somaliland

British South Africa Company

Brunei

Burma

Canada

Cape Colony

Ceylon

Cook Islands

Cyprus

Dominica

East India Company

Fiji

Gambia

Gilbert and Ellice Islands

Gold Coast

Grenada

Heligoland

Hong Kong

India

Ionian Islands

Ireland

Jamaica

Kenya

Labuan

Lagos

Leeward Islands

Liu Kung Tau

Malacca

Federated Malay States

Unfederated Malay States

Malaya

Maldives

Malta

Mauritius

Mosquito Coast

Natal

Nauru

New Hebrides

Newfoundland

New South Wales

New Zealand

Niger Coast Protectorate

Nigeria

Niue

North Borneo

Northern Nigeria

Northern Rhodesia

Nyasaland

Orange River Colony

Palestine

Penang

Queensland

Rhodesia

Federation of Rhodesia and Nyasaland

Royal Niger Company

Saint Christopher, Nevis and Anguilla

Saint Kitts and Nevis

Saint Lucia

Saint Vincent and the Grenadines

Sarawak

Seychelles

Sierra Leone

Singapore

Solomon Islands

South Africa

South Australia

Southern Nigeria

Southern Rhodesia

Straits Settlements

Sudan

Swaziland

Tanganyika

Tasmania

Tonga

Transvaal

Trinidad and Tobago

Turks and Caicos Islands

Uganda

Victoria Colony

Weiheiwei

West Indies Federation

West Pacific High Commissioner

Western Australia

Western Samoa

Windward Islands

Witu Protectorate

Zanzibar

HOW TO MAKE THE PERFECT YORKSHIRE PUDDINGS

113g (4oz) of plain flour, 2 eggs, just under 280ml (1/2 pint) of milk and a pinch of salt, whisked together into a batter. Add lard to the baking tin and heat up to 250°C (482°F, gas mark 8). Cook at the top of the oven for 15 minutes.

25 ELEMENTARY SHERLOCK HOLMES ADVENTURES

A Scandal In Bohemia

The Red-Headed League

The Case Of Identity

The Boscombe Valley Mystery

The Five Orange Pips

The Man With The Twisted Lip

The Adventure Of The Blue Carbuncle

The Adventure Of The Speckled Band

The Adventure Of The Engineer's Thumb

The Adventure Of The Noble Bachelor

The Adventure Of The Beryl Coronet

The Adventure Of The Copper Beeches

The Adventure Of The Silver Blaze

The Adventure Of The Cardboard Box

The Adventure Of The Yellow Face

The Adventure Of The Stockbroker's Clerk

The Adventure Of The 'Gloria Scott'

The Adventure Of The Musgrave Ritual

The Adventure Of The Reigate Squire

The Adventure Of The Crooked Man

The Adventure Of The Resident Patient

The Adventure Of The Greek Interpreter

The Adventure Of The Naval Treaty

The Adventure Of The Final Problem

GONE BUT NOT FORGOTTEN: DEFUNCT BRITISH BRAND NAMES

Marathon, Opal Fruits, Jif, Windscale, Mercury, BSB, Cellnet, OnDigital, Players, Omo, Atari, Oil of Ulay, Air UK, Toffo, British Caledonian, Pepsodent.

DICK WHITTINGTON – THE TRUTH

Most English people are familiar with the legend of Dick Whittington and his cat. The legend is that Dick Whittington, a poor country boy, came to London with his cat seeking his fortune. When he reached Highgate Hill, he lost heart and turned to go back home. Then he heard the bells of London ringing out, saying, 'Turn again, Dick Whittington, three-times Lord Mayor of London.'

In reality, Richard Whittington, four-times Mayor of London, was born in Pauntley, Gloucestershire, sometime around 1350, and was the youngest son of a local landowner. He arrived in London, was apprenticed as a Mercer (a dealer in cloth), becoming a wealthy and successful merchant, and made mayor of London by Richard II in 1397. Under Henry IV, Whittington was elected mayor for a further three terms, 1397–8, 1406–7 and 1419–20. He also lent King Henry considerable sums of money and, in return, sat on many Royal Commissions.

Richard Whittington died in March 1423. His estate of £5000 (an amount equivalent to several million now) was used for charitable purposes. These included rebuilding Newgate Prison, the building of the first library in Guildhall, work on St Bartholomew's Hospital and establishing almshouses for poor people.

If he had a cat, then nobody knows.

WINNERS OF THE TURNER PRIZE FOR CONTEMPORARY ART

Since its inception in 1995, the Turner Prize has become Britain's most controversial art award. Winning works have included a halved cow in formaldehyde and a picture of the Virgin Mary in elephant dung.

1995: Damien Hirst ('Mother And Child Divided')

1996: Douglas Gordon ('Confessions Of A Justified Sinner')

1997: Gillian Wearing ('Sixty Minute Silence')

1998: Chris Offili ('The Virgin Mary')

1999: Steve McQueen ('Assorted Video Work')

2000: Wolfgang Tillmans ('Concorde')

2001: Martin Creed ('Lights Going On And Off')

2002: Keith Tyson ('Kentucky Fried Chicken Menu Cast In Lead')

OUT OF THIS WORLD: GATESHEAD'S ANGEL OF THE NORTH

Sculpted by Andrew Gormley, since its erection near Gateshead, Tyne and Wear in 1996, the Angel has become a landmark. It is also:

- the largest sculpture in Britain

- believed to be the largest angel sculpture in the world

- one of the most viewed pieces of art in the world – seen by more than one person every second, 90,000 every day or 33 million every year

- bigger than a Boeing 757 or 767 jet and almost the same as a Jumbo jet, with a 54m (175ft) wingspan

- 20m (65ft) high – the height of a five-storey building or four double decker buses

- 200 tonnes (220 tons) in weight – the body 100 tonnes (110 tons) and the wings 50 tonnes (55 tons) each

THE FIRST NIGHT OF THE LONDON BLITZ

Between five and six o'clock on the evening of Saturday 7 September 1940, some 320 German bombers, supported by over 600 fighters, flew up the Thames and proceeded to bomb Woolwich Arsenal, Beckton gasworks, a large number of docks, West Ham power station, and then the city, Westminster and Kensington. The area between North Woolwich Road and the Thames was almost destroyed, and the population of Silvertown was surrounded by fire and had to be evacuated by water. At 8:10pm some 250 bombers resumed the attack which was maintained until 4:30am on Sunday. They caused 9 conflagrations, 59 large fires and nearly 1,000 lesser fires. Three main line railway termini were put out of action, and 430 persons killed and some 1,600 seriously injured.

SUPERSONIC BRITS

The Land Speed record has been broken many times, but mainly by Britons. In 1997, Richard Noble's 1983 record of 1,013 kph (633 mph) was beaten by Thrust Super Sonic Car, driven by RAF pilot Andy Green at 1,142 kph (714 mph). On Wednesday 15 October of that year, Thrust SSC became the first 'car' to break the Sound Barrier setting the new record at 1,220.354 kph (762.721 mph).

THE TOP 10 BRITONS (ACCORDING TO BBC TV VIEWERS IN 2003)

Winston Churchill

Isambard Kingdom Brunel

Princess Diana

Charles Darwin

William Shakespeare

Isaac Newton

Queen Elizabeth I

John Lennon

Horatio Nelson

Oliver Cromwell

THE KNOWLEDGE

In order to gain their licence, potential London taxi drivers have to pass The Knowledge. This is a proven thorough knowledge of London, including the location of streets, squares, clubs, hospitals, hotels, theatres, government and public buildings, railway stations, police stations, courts, diplomatic buildings, important places of worship, cemeteries, crematoria, parks and open spaces, sports and leisure centres, places of learning, restaurants and historic buildings; in fact everything you need to know to be able to take passengers to their destinations by the most direct routes.

BRITAIN'S OLDEST BREWERY

Shepherd Neame, regarded as Britain's oldest brewery, began in 1698 when Captain Richard Marsh, Mayor of Faversham, Kent, founded a brewery over an artesian well in the town. In 1741 the brewery was acquired by Samuel Shepherd, a member of a prominent land-owning family and already active for some years in Faversham as a maltster. With a growing population to serve, Faversham was becoming an increasingly important brewing town when Samuel Shepherd was joined in the business by his sons Julius and John. It was at this stage that the family began buying pubs, several of which are still owned by the company today. As various partners joined the firm, so the name changed to Shepherd & Hilton, Shepherd & Mares and, finally, when John Mares died and 28-year-old Percy Beale Neame joined the partnership in 1864, Shepherd Neame.

GETTING AWAY FROM IT ALL: BRITAIN'S FAVOURITE HOLIDAY DESTINATIONS

Spain

France

Greece

USA

Italy

Irish Republic

Portugal

Cyprus

Netherlands

Turkey

Caribbean

Mexico

Croatia

Bulgaria

Dubai

South Africa

UK

THE GOLDEN AGE? 10 CLASSIC BRITISH SITCOMS FROM THE 1970S

1 *Fawlty Towers*

2 *Love Thy Neighbour*

3 *The Good Life*

4 *On The Buses*

5 *Up Pompeii*

6 *The Fall And Rise Of Reginald Perrin*

7 *George And Mildred*

8 *Porridge*

9 *Rising Damp*

10 *It Ain't Half Hot Mum*

BEACH FLAGS

British beaches rely on a flag system to ensure the safety of visitors. Red and yellow flags indicate a designated bathing area for swimmers, boogie and body boards. Black and white flags indicate a safe area for all surfcraft over 1.5m (5ft) in length. (This includes canoes, windsurfers, etc.) The red flag indicates that the sea conditions are dangerous. Never enter the sea when the red flag is flying.

A VERY BRITISH SPY: ACTORS WHO HAVE PLAYED JAMES BOND

David Niven *(Casino Royale)*

Sean Connery *(Dr No, Goldfinger, From Russia With Love, You Only Live Twice, Thunderball, Diamonds Are Forever, Never Say Never Again)*

George Lazenby *(On Her Majesty's Secret Service)*

Roger Moore *(Live And Let Die, The Man With The Golden Gun, The Spy Who Loved Me, Moonraker, For Your Eyes Only, Octopussy, A View To A Kill)*

Timothy Dalton *(The Living Daylights, Licence To Kill)*

Pierce Brosnan *(Goldeneye, Tomorrow Never Dies, The World Is Not Enough, Die Another Day)*

SIGN LANGUAGE – SOME BIZARRE SIGNS FOUND IN THE BRITISH WORKPLACE

- Would the person who took the stepladder please return it or further steps will be taken.

- After tea break, staff must empty the teapot and stand upside down on the draining board.

- Smarts is the most exclusive disco in town. Everybody welcome.

- We repair what your husband fixed.

- Have your ears pierced and get an extra pair to take home.

- Toilet out of order, please use floor below.

- Bargain basement upstairs.

- Seafood brought in by customers will not be entertained.

- Horse manure 50p-a-bag, ready packed. 20p-a-bag, do it yourself.

INDEX

A1 road 89
accommodation used by foreign visitors 44
air journeys, longest from the UK 18
aircraft, crash landing on road 20
airline flight, shortest UK scheduled 94
airport, world's busiest 7
airports 41
Alnwick Castle 109
alphabet, Old English 161
Alton Towers 53, 73
Angel of the North, Gateshead 188
Appleby-in-Westmoreland horse fair 80
aquarium, world's deepest 89
areas of British countries 63
army, definition 99
army, private, Britain's only 117
art, Turner Prize winners 187
Arthur, King 167
astronaut, first British 98
Athelhampton Hall, Dorset 84
Atholl, Duke of 117
attractions, top (see *visitor attractions, top*)
Australia, convicts sent to 113

bagpipe parts 122–3
Baird, John Logie 50, 75
balloon festival, Northampton 53
Baltic Centre for Contemporary Art, Gateshead 150
Bass Rock 160
Bath, Roman spa baths 75
battle, last on English soil 68
battles, England vs Scotland, since 1066: 100–1
beach flags 191
Beatles, The 80 (see also *Lennon, John*; *Liverpool, Eleanor Rigby statue*; *Liverpool, Penny Lane connections*; *London, Abbey Road'*)
birthplaces 79
Marylebone locations 105
bed habits, most irritating 171
beer consumption 82 (see also *brewery, Britain's oldest*)
beer-drinking terms 153
belching in public 75

Bell, Alexander Graham, wife and mother 56
Berkeley Castle 69
Berwick-upon-Tweed 87
Big Ben 91
bingo facts 107
birds 30, 98, 138, 167
Birmingham (see also *Bourneville*; *Spaghetti Junction*; *White Swan, Harborne, Birmingham*)
canals 52
Blackburn, Lancs 67
Blackpool, Lancs 95
history 69
illuminations, celebrities switching on 76–7
Blackpool Tower 151
Blarney Stone 113
'Blighty', meaning of 66
blue plaques 50
boat race, oldest 20
Bodleian Library 66
Bodmin Moor 45
Bolan, Marc 79
Boleyn, Anne 50
Bond, James 134
actors playing 191
bookshop, Foyle's 38, 90
Bosworth Hall, Leics 84
Boudicca 65
Bourne windmill, Cambs 10
Bournville, nr Birmingham 175
Bowie, David, *Ziggy Stardust And The Spiders From Mars* album cover 37
Boy Scouts, first camp 35
Bramshill House, Hants 84
brand names, defunct British 186
Branson, Richard 142
brewery, Britain's oldest 189
bridges
cantilever, Britain's longest 95, 96
Clifton Suspension 54
Forth Rail 90, 95, 96
Millennium 69, 139
Thames, in London 69
Brighton 40
marina 44, 96
Volks Electric Railway 10

Bristol, Clifton Suspension Bridge 54
Bristol, oldest public house 62
British Empire 41, 184–5
British people, useless facts 43
Britons, top ten 189
Brooke, Roy 81
Brownsea Island, Poole Harbour 35
Buckingham Palace 89
building, oldest municipal 72
buildings, record breaking 22
buildings, tallest 16, 32
burials, excavated Saxons 171
burials at sea 27
Burke, William, and William Hare 172
Burns, Robert, 'Ode Tae A Mouse'
    12–13
Burton Agnes Hall, Humberside 84
Busby Stoop Inn, Sand Hutton, N
    Yorks 24
buses, first 23
Butlins Holiday Camp, first 82

caber-tossing 7
cable car, Britain's longest 116
cabs, hansom 23
Cadbury's chocolate 175
Caerphilly Castle 51
Cambridge University 36
cameras, speeding, top ten police
    forces 23
Campbell, Alex 39
canal, first in Britain 78 (see also *ship
    canal, oldest*)
canals in Birmingham 52
Canary Wharf, London 16
Canterbury, Kent 20
Cardiff, Millennium Stadium 43
cars, most popular/unpopular 180
castle, first designed for artillery 74
castle, largest 22
cathedral, only domed 21
cathedral city, smallest in Britain 79
caves 59
    Chislehurst 20
Cenotaph Ceremony 16
centre of Britain, geographical 38
Cerne Abbas Giant 73
Channel Tunnel 66, 96
Channel Tunnel Rail Link 31
cheeses 71
Chester, Roodee horse race 81

chicken tikka masala 139
Chinese gateway, largest in Europe
    78, 96
Chippenham, Wilts 45
Chislehurst Caves, Kent 20
Churchill, Winston, speech 150
cities, furthest by air from the UK 18
cities, major UK, average IQ of
    population 86
city, Britain's smallest 130
city, first with more than one million
    population 54
city, oldest in Britain 31
city populations 19
city status, loss 62
Civil War 51
Clifton Suspension Bridge 54
coastal erosion 160
Cochrane, Eddie 45
cock fighting 103
cockney rhyming slang 162
cockneys 21
coinage, defunct UK 181
Colchester, Essex 65
colonels, retired, in Hythe 66
competitions, eccentric 11
constituencies, political 110
    smallest majorities 121
Continent, nearest point to 115
counties 140
county, smallest 55
Courtier's House, Oxon 84
Covent Garden 98
culinary statistics 19
Culloden, Battle of 127
Cumbria, top attractions 107, 121
curry 79, 99

Dartmoor 45
Dartmouth Castle 74
Darwin, Charles 169
Deal, Kent, shipwrecks 117
death, last serviceman in World War I
    43
death, last words before 148–9
death, most common causes 178
deaths, rock 'n' roll 111
Defoe, Daniel 117
dialling codes, obscure 146
Dickens, Charles 50, 103
disaster, peacetime, Britain's worst 183

divorces (1999) 97
Doggett, Thomas 20
dogs, Rottweiler 159
dogs, UK's most popular 161
dogs' names, top ten 180
Dome, Millennium 114, 179–80
Dove pub, Hammersmith 29
Dover, Kent 115
Downing Street, No 10: 125
driving on left-hand side of road 55
Dunmow Flitch 67
Durham Cathedral 109

email, first sent by Queen Elizabeth II
    55
Ealing Studios 58
earthquakes (since 1901) 154
Eden project 71
Edinburgh
    Burke and Hare 172
    Greyfriars Bobby 144–5
Edward II, King 69
Edwards, Richey 44
'Electric Brae' (Croy Brae) 35
Elizabeth II, Queen 176–7 (see also
    royal facts; royal quotes)
    email 55
    Golden Jubilee 120–1
Eros statue 117
escalators, first 40
Essex English, A–Z of 154
Essex Girl jokes 22
Eton Wall Game 26–7
Europe, Britain's best in 96
Eurostar trains 31
Exeter 72
Exmoor 45
Eyam, Derbys 53

Falcon Hotel, Castle Ashby, Northants
    24
farming facts 47
figurines, Royal Doulton 20
films (see also Bond, James; Ealing
    Studios; Pinewood Studios)
    A Hard Day's Night 105
    Harry Potter locations 109
    London locations 8, 13
    Madness Of King George III, The
        167
    shot in Scotland 168

fingers, six 50
fish and chip shop, world's largest 81,
    90
fish and chips 124
floods (1953) 183
'Flower Of Scotland' 93
flowers, national 128
follies, ten great British 183
food facts 47, 99
    brains and bacon 123
    cheeses 71
    chicken tikka masala 139
    consumption in restaurants, etc 19
    curry 79, 99
    fast food, most popular 124
    fish and chip shop, world's largest
        81, 90
    fish and chips 124
    haggis ingredients 34
    HP Sauce 178
    London restaurants, etc 150
    meal, Britain's favourite 79, 139
    sandwiches 96
    sausages 141
    sweets, boiled 82
    Yorkshire puddings 185
foreign visitors, accommodation 44
forest, largest in Britain 85
fort, Iron Age, largest in northwest
    Europe 132
Forth Rail Bridge 90, 95, 96
Foyle's bookshop, Charing Cross Rd
    38, 90
funerals, burials at sea 27

galleries, most visited 24 (see also
    London, visitor attractions, top)
gangsters, East End 136
gardens, top ten visited 27
Gateshead
    Angel of the North 188
    Baltic Centre for Contemporary Art
        150
'Geordie', origin of expression 88
George I, King 135
George V, King 111, 171
Giant's Causeway, Co Antrim 175
Glastonbury 45
Gloucestershire 163
GMT 60 (see also radio, pips
    time signal)

Goathland Station, N Yorks 109
gorge, largest 72
Grand National, first 81
Grantchester, Lady 142
Gravesend, Kent 167
Gray, Hugh 39
Great Exhibition 159
Great Orme, Llandudno 116
Gretna Green 34
grouse 167
Guiseley, W Yorks, Harry Ramsden chippie 81, 90
Gunpowder Plot 176

habits, bad 75
haggis ingredients 34
Halloween 110
Hampton Court maze 7
hanging, last in Britain 78
hangman, most prolific 20th century 183
Hard Day's Night, A 105
Harrod's, London 40
Harry Potter locations 109
Hatchett Inn, Bristol 62
haunted hotels and inns 24–5
haunted houses 84–5
Heathrow Airport 7, 90
heliports 41
Hendrix, Jimi 56, 116
heritage sites, visited by overseas holidaymakers 65
highest point in Britain 67
Highland Games, unexpected places where held 144 (see also caber-tossing)
Hinduja, Sri and Gopi 142
HMV, first shop 56
hobbies, unusual 36–7
holiday destinations, Britain's favourite 190
Holmes, Sherlock 50, 103, 186
honours system 119
Hope-Jones, Frank 112–13
Hopkins, Matthew (Witchfinder General) 17
horse fair, largest 80
horse racing, first race 81
horse racing, first Grand National 81
hotel, Britain's most expensive 124
hotels, haunted 24–5

house, largest private 22
house, oldest 22
house plants, most popular 52
houses, top UK 88
HP Sauce 178
Hull, The Deep 87, 89
Hythe, Kent 66

Ightham Mote, Kent 85
industry, British production 44
inns, haunted 24–5
Inspector Morse 62
insurance against going to hell 110
invasion, Britain's last 99
invasions, southern 113
inventors 10
Ipswich, Suffolk 174
IQ of population in major UK cities 86
Ireland, patron saint 82, 116
Irish living in London 62
islands off UK coast 159
Isle of Wight 15, 159

Jack the Ripper 153
jokes, Englishman, Irishman, Scotsman 101
jokes, Essex Girl 22
jokes, mother-in-law 37
Jonson, Ben 56

karaoke machine 81
Kennedy, John F 50
Kent, most-visited tourist attraction 20
Kew Gardens 26, 27, 90, 116
Kielder Water, Northumberland 85, 96
Kray, Ronnie and Reggie 136

lake, man-made, largest in Europe 85, 96
Lakeside Shopping Centre, Thurrock 38
'Land Of My Fathers' 124–5
Land Speed record, recent British winners 188
Land's End to John O'Groats journey 65
Lanesborough Hotel 124
language, second, EU countries without 160
languages spoken in London 81
laws, unusual 126–7

Lennon, John 19, 67
Lewis, Jerry Lee and Myra 25
Lewis, Joseph 142
library, oldest 66
life expectancy 56
Lighthouse, Eddystone 149
lighthouse, tallest 72
lighthouse builders, British 161
'Limeys' 53
Liverpool 86
  Beatles birthplaces 79
  Cathedral 90, 96, 106
  Eleanor Rigby statue 78
  Mersey Tunnel 30
  Penny Lane connections 80
  Scouse 79
Llandudno, Great Orme 116
Llanfair PG, Anglesey 129
Loch Ness monster 39
London
  Abbey Road 143
  221b Baker St 103
  Bar Italia, Frith St 75
  Berwick St 143
  Big Ben 91
  Blitz, first night 188
  blue plaques 50
  boat race, Doggett's Coat and
  Badge 20
  Buckingham Palace 89
  buildings, tallest 16, 32
  buses, first 23
  Canary Wharf 16
  Catholics living in 62
  cockneys 21
  Covent Garden 98
  9 Curzon Place, Flat 12: 111
  distances from 9
  Dove pub, Hammersmith 29
  10 Downing Street 125
  'Exotic Gherkin' building 16, 176
  Foyle's bookshop, Charing Cross
  Rd 38, 90
  Great Fire 17
  hansom cabs, first 23
  Harrod's 40
  Heddon St, telephone box 37
  Irish living in 62
  Kew Gardens 26, 27, 90, 116
  languages spoken 81
  Madame Tussaud's 159

Marc Bolan sites 79
Marylebone 105
Mayfair 72
MI6 headquarters 13
Millennium Dome 114, 179
movie locations 8, 13, 105
musical top 40: 57
Nelson's Column 13
parks 93
Piccadilly Circus, Eros statue 117
population 54, 158, 167
restaurant cuisines 17
restaurants etc. 150
St Paul's Cathedral 21, 96
Samarkand Hotel 56
Savoy Hotel 131
Savoy Theatre 97
sewers 170
Thames Barrier 10, 90
Thames bridges and tunnels 69
Tower 74
Trafalgar Square 9, 13
traffic speed 167
Trooping the Colour 130
Tyburn Tree and Convent 130
visitor attractions, top 9, 23
Waterloo station 90
Westbury Hotel, Conduit St 25
Westminster Abbey 56, 92
London Eye 32
London Underground 42, 90
Lottery, National (UK Lotto) 132, 180
lowest point in Britain 67
Lundy Island 48–9

M25 motorway 40
Madness 174
Madness Of King George III, The 167
mail-order shopping 134
Mama Cass 111
'man', Britain's oldest 115
man, Britain's oldest 157
Manchester
  Chinatown, Imperial Arch 78, 96
  Strangeways prison 78
Manic Street Preachers' guitarist 44
Manningtree, Essex 17
marina, Europe's largest man-made
  44, 96
marriage, Dunmow Flitch award 67
marriage vows 118

marriages (1999) 97
marriages, average age 103
Martini, making, like James Bond 134
Marx, Karl 50
Maumbury Rings 72
Mayfair 72
maze, Hampton Court 7
maze, largest 72
meal, Britain's favourite 79, 139
medicines, world's bestselling 103
Members of Parliament, salary 95
men, tall 177
Mersey Tunnel 30
MI6 headquarters, London 13
Midlands, top attractions 76, 89
military mottos 151
Mittal, Lakshmi 143
mobile phones, number of 31
Mompesson, William 53
monarchs, English 32–3 (see also
    Arthur, King; *Edward II, King*;
    Elizabeth II, Queen; *George I,
    King*; *George V, King*; *royal facts*;
    royal quotes)
monument, Neolithic, Ballylumford
    Dolmen 145
monuments, historic, top UK 88
Moon, Keith 111
Moores family 142
moors, southwest England 45
Morgan, Able Seaman Richard 43
Morris, William Richard 20
Morris dance 163
Morse, Inspector 62
mother-in-law jokes 37
motorway, M25: 40
motorways, Spaghetti Junction 83
mound, artificial, largest in Europe 56
mountains, Britain's highest 110
mountains, Munro 15
movies (see *films*)
municipal building, oldest 72
Munro, Sir Hector and mountains 15
murder methods, most common 140
murderers, Britain's most prolific
    168–9
museums, most visited 24 (see also
    London, visitor attractions, top)
museums, sports 118
museums for a very rainy day 9
music retailer, world's largest 56

names, first, top ten 105
Nash, Richard Beau 109
National Anthem 64 (see also *'Flower
    Of Scotland'*; *'Land Of My
    Fathers'*)
national emblems 128
national parks 106
nationalities, predominant, in UK 70
Navy, British, Admiral of the 177
Nelson's Column, Trafalgar Square
    13
New Forest 35
Newcastle-upon-Tyne, origin of
    'Geordie' 88
Northampton racecourse, annual
    balloon festival 53
Northern Ireland
    Ballylumford Dolmen (Neolithic
        monument) 145
    Giant's Causeway, Co Antrim 175
Northumberland, top attractions 143,
    145
northwest, top attractions 131, 137
nose picking 75
Nottingham Magistrates Court 52
novels inspired by southwest moors
    45
nuclear bunkers, Cold War 136
Numan, Gary 20
numbers, random, Britain in 112
nursery rhymes 182

Oasis 143
observation wheel, tallest 32
office facts 175
Old Ferryboat Inn, Holywell, Cambs
    24
Olympics 2012, planned venues 126
optical illusion 35
Orkney, shortest scheduled UK airline
    flight 94
Orkney, Skara Brae 70
Orwell, George, and tea making 55
Oxford, Morris motors 20
Oxford English Dictionary 74
Oxford University 36, 65
    Bodleian Library 66

Parliament, Members of, salary 95
patron saints (see *St Andrew*; *St
    David*; *St George*; *St Patrick*)

Penfound Manor, Cornwall 85
Percival, Spencer 178–9
pets 160
pharmaceutical companies 103
Philip, Prince 177
phobias 114
phrases, baffling 67–8 (see also
  sayings)
Pinewood Studios 27
place names
  history 155–7
  longest 129
  numerical 61
  pronouncing 58
  unfortunate 94
  unusual 62
places, grottiest 129
Plague, Great 53
plants, house, most popular 52
plaques, blue 50
Poets Laureate 135, 170
police forces, with most speeding
  cameras 23
political parties 102
Poole Harbour 35, 163, 166
population (2003) 83
population, first city with more than
  one million 54
population, world's 15
population density in England 83
populations of cities 19
port, Britain's oldest 163
Portmeirion 49
poteen 137
Potteries 75
pounds, abbreviation (weight) 91
pregnancies, teenage 56
Presley, Elvis, UK visit 91
Prime Minister, contacting 181
Prime Minister, only assassinated 178
prison population 177 (see also
  Australia, convicts sent to)
Prisoner, The 49
prostitutes, UK spending on 82
pub games, traditional 152
pubs 174 (see also inns, most
  haunted)
  highest in Britain 82
  names, oddest 104–5
  names, UK's most popular 152
  oldest in Britain 38

Purbeck, Dorset 166
Pythouse, Wilts 85

radio, BBC World Service, 135
radio, pips time signal 112–13
rail service, passenger, fastest 31
railway, Britain's only rack and pinion
  134
railway, oldest electric 10
Raleigh, Sir Walter 53
Ramsden, Harry 81, 90
rap culture, terms with origins in 158
Rausing, Hans 142
record breakers, southwest 72
record breakers, southeast 22
religions in Britain 70
Remembrance Day, Cenotaph
  Ceremony 16
resort, designer 35
restaurants, cuisines in London 17
restaurants etc, in London 150
richest top ten, Britain's 142–3
Ripon, Yorks 31
  Wakeman 86
rivers, longest in Britain 35
roads
  A, Britain's most dangerous 174
  A, Britain's longest 89
  A1: 89
  A3051, Botley to Winchester 20
  driving on left-hand side 55
  'Electric Brae' (Croy Brae) 35
robberies, Britain's biggest 179
robin 138
Rochester, Kent 62
  Charles Dickens 103
rock 'n' roll deaths 111
rock stars, richest 51
Roman palace, largest 22
Roman remain, tallest 22
Roman town names 63
Royal Doulton figurines 20
royal facts 115
royal quotes 111
royalty, addressing 14
Rutland 55

Sainsbury, Lord, and family 142
St Alban 67
St Albans, Ye Olde Fighting Cocks
  pub 38

St Andrew 40–1
St Cuthbert 82
St David 131
St David's, Pembs 130, 131
St George 97
St Kilda (island) 98
St Patrick 116
St Paul's Cathedral, London 21, 96
salaries, best annual, by postcode 133
Salford Docks (Quays) 149
Sandwich, Fourth Earl of 96
sausages 141
Savoy Hotel, London 131
Savoy Theatre 97
sayings 46–7 (see also phrases, baffling)
school, oldest 22
Schroder, Bruno, and family 142
Scole Inn, nr Diss, Norfolk 25
Scotland, patron saint 40–1
Scott, Sir Peter 30
Scouse 79
Scouts, Boy, first camp 35
scurvy 53
sea bar, longest 72
seabird colony, Europe's most important 98
Sedgemoor, Battle of 68
Severn Bridge Service Station 44
sex, first, average age for 56
Sex Pistols, The 52
Shakespeare, William 49, 74
Sharman, Helen 98
Shepherd Neame brewery 189
ship canal, oldest 72
shipping forecast 171
shopping centre, largest 38
signs, bizarre workplace 191
Silbury Hill, Wilts 56, 96
Skara Brae, Orkney 70
Skegness, Butlins Holiday Camp 82
slang words and phrases 46–7 (see also cockney rhyming slang)
slavery, abolition 110
sleuths, British literary 182 (see also Holmes, Sherlock)
Slimbridge wildfowl centre 30
snoring 171
Snowdon Mountain Railway 134
Soros, George 142

southeast, top attractions 31, 38 (see also London, visitor attractions, top)
southeast record breaking buildings/town 22
Southend-on-Sea, Essex 31, 35
southwest, top attractions 52, 59
southwest record breakers 72
Spaghetti Junction 83
speeding cameras, top ten police forces 23
sporting competitions, eccentric 11
sports museums 118
Staffordshire, potteries 75
Stonehenge 61 (see also Maumbury Rings)
Stratford-upon-Avon, Holy Trinity Church 49
structural engineering failure, worst 30
studio sound stage, largest 27
Studios, Ealing 58
suicides, Severn Bridge 44
Sunningdale, Tittenhurst Park Estate mansion 19
sweets, boiled 82
syllable -ough 97

tall men 177
Tarn Hill Inn, N Yorks 82
tattoo, royal 171
taxi drivers (London), The Knowledge 189
Tay Bridge Disaster 30
tea consumption 134
tea making, George Orwell's tips 55
telephone box on Ziggy Stardust And The Spiders From Mars album cover 37
telephones, number of 31
television
    classic 1970s sitcoms 190
    Coronation Street stars 88
    first demonstrated 75
    Inspector Morse 62
    ITV's first night's schedule 147
    Prisoner, The 49
    Top Of The Pops 78
Thames, River 170
Thames Barrier 10, 90
Thatcher, Margaret, quotes 181

theatre, first lit by electricity 97
theatre, oldest 72
theme-park rides 28–9, 53, 73
times, world, when 12:00 GMT 60
tobacco smoke, weight 53
toilet, euphemisms 126
Top o' the Hill figurine, Royal Doulton 20
Top Of The Pops 78
tossing a caber 7
tourism 41, 95
tourist attractions (see visitor attractions)
Tower of London, animals 74
town, oldest in UK 22
town names, Roman 63
towns, top tourist 133
trade unions 108–9
trading nation, world's fifth largest 109
Trafalgar Square, London 9, 13
Trooping the Colour 130
Tunbridge Wells 109
tunnels, Thames, in London 69
Turner Prize winners 187
Tussaud, Madame 159

underwear, changing 75
Union Flag 18, 49
university, oldest 65

visitor attractions, top, in Britain (free) 91, 138
    Cumbria 121
    London 23
    Midlands 89
    Northumberland 145
    northwest 137
    southeast 38
    southwest 59
    Yorkshire 170
visitor attractions, top, in Britain (paid) 87 (see also theme-park rides)
    Cumbria 107
    London 9
    Midlands 76
    Northumberland 143
    northwest 131
    southeast 31
    southwest 52
    Yorkshire 158

visitors, overseas, accommodation used by 44
visitors, overseas, most popular pastime 65
vocabulary, average person's 74
Volks Electric Railway, Brighton 10

Wales, patron saint 131
Wales and sheep 177
walks, Britain's long-distance 164–6
walls, dry-stone 163
war, shortest in the world 103
Water Sports Centre, National, Holme Pierrepoint 55
Waterloo station 90
weather, official climate 40
weather records 172
websites, pornographic 62
weddings, Gretna Green 34
Wells, Somerset 79
Westbury Hotel, Conduit St, London 25
Westminster, Duke of 142
Westminster Abbey 56, 92
Weston, Garfield, and family 142
Weston Manor Hotel, Weston-on-the-Green, Oxon 25
White Swan, Harborne, Birmingham 25
Whittington, Dick 187
wildfowl centre, world's largest 30
Winchester Cathedral 96, 167
wind, Beaufort Scale 172–3
wind, passing 75
windmill, Bourn, Cambs 10
Winstanley, Henry 149
Witchfinder General (Matthew Hopkins) 17
woman, Britain's oldest 160
woodland coverage in UK 101
world beaters, Britain's 90
World War I, last serviceman to die 43
Wren, Sir Christopher 21

Ye Olde Fighting Cocks pub, St Albans 38
Yorkshire, top attractions 158, 170
Yorkshire puddings 185

Zanzibar, war against 103